ABOUT THE AUTHOR

B. Ryan is a writer and researcher. She is author of *Feminist of Knowing* (NIACE, 2001) and co-editor of *Women and Edu- in Ireland* (MACE, 1999). She lives in Celbridge, County Kil- and is currently an associate member of staff at The Centre dult and Community Education, NUI Maynooth.

Balancing Your Life

A practical guide to work, time, money and happiness

Anne B. Ryan

The Liffey Press

Published by
The Liffey Press
Ashbrook House
10 Main Street, Raheny
Dublin 5, Ireland
www.theliffeypress.com

A catalogue record of this book is
available from the British Library.

ISBN 1-904148-20-4

Printed in the Republic of Ireland by Colour Books Ltd.

CONTENTS

ACKNOWLEDGEMENTS

First, I thank everybody who told me their stories for this book. I hope I have done justice to your experiences. I dedicate the book to all of you, whether your story appears in the final text or not.

I am deeply grateful to John Quinn for writing the foreword for this book and for his kind words.

I talked to many other people about the ideas in this book, and every conversation has given me food for thought. Thanks to all whose words of advice have guided me; your voices are part of this book. In particular, I have benefited enormously from the collegiality and friendship of Bríd Connolly and David McCormack. Mags Boland, Trish Bowler, Bernie Browne, Kim Close, Martin Close, Tom Collins, Linda Connolly, Anne Gallagher, Breda Gibney, Maureen Gillespie, Andrew Herring, Julia Hogan, Ike Jacob, Louise Keane, Stephanie Larkin, Liz Leonard, Anne Love, Mary Lally, Peter McIlwaine, Mac MacLachlan, Mary Murray, Edel O'Kennedy, Mary Quinn, Áine Ryan, Mary B. Ryan, Hilary Tovey, Derek Walsh and Penny Wilson have helped in myriad ways. As always, my sisters, Mary Ryan, Helen Ryan and Joan Ryan, my brother Tony Ryan, and my parents, Evelyn Ryan and Brendan Ryan, have provided a wealth of ideas and support.

I have read many books and articles on balanced living, simplicity, downshifting, and setting goals and priorities, all of which are mentioned in the bibliography. I am grateful to the writers who have gone before me, and whose ideas I have used and built on.

At The Liffey Press, Brian Langan was a very helpful editor and both he and David Givens were constructive and encouraging at all times.

Last to be mentioned as usual, but only because he is first in my heart, I thank Frank Savino for his part in the creation of this book. Together, in all the complicated and sometimes unsettling realities of balance-seeking, we shape our dreams.

FOREWORD

In March 2001, I chaired a seminar in the National Concert Hall, Dublin. The theme was "Balancing Your Life" and the speaker was Charles Handy. His opening remark was that there was something ironic in the fact that 700 people had given up their Saturday morning to try and find balance in their lives! He had a point, but the presence of the 700 indicated the growing strength of a movement that is asking: what is enough? A simple question. Finding the answer is a complex process.

Anne B. Ryan has sensed the growth of that movement and in writing this book she offers a depth of practical guidance towards breaking out of the work–earn–spend culture. By adapting philosophies and traditions from around the globe and wedding these to case studies of Irish "downshifters" and "longtimers", Anne Ryan has put "Balancing Your Life" in an Irish context and, in doing so, offers positive and constructive guidelines for those who are seeking balance in their lives.

This book is not and cannot be a blueprint for any one individual. As the author reminds us, "enough is creative". We shape our own lives, create our own dreams, so the reader may draw from this book what applies to their situation and will hopefully build on that. And balance, we are reminded, is a process not a place. It is a journey of discovery and it can be a lonely journey. Honesty is the hallmark of the interviews in this book. The case studies are real; they are not the stuff of television fiction, or even of "reality" television. These are people who thought "outside the box", made hard decisions and broke out of the work–earn–spend culture. They will provoke a lot of thought for even the mildly interested reader.

Anne Ryan's practical suggestions on such issues as "mindful spending" and using time wisely bring to mind Einstein's famous dictum: "not everything that is countable counts and not everything that counts is countable". If we are to achieve balance in our lives, we need to rethink how we use both money and time. Personally, I applaud a book that says "we need to revive the term laziness in a positive way" and "children benefit from doing nothing and learning to daydream".

But there is much more to applaud in this book. It is practical and well-grounded without being prescriptive and it is quite simply a good read and, thankfully, jargon-free. Anne Ryan is honest enough to acknowledge that having scanned the book you may decide it is not for you — just now (and if you have not time to scan it you have a serious problem!). Even so, there may just be the seed of an idea in these pages that may grow within you at some future date. In the words of Paolo Freire, "we make the road by walking" — and we begin to walk by taking baby steps.

Many of us will remember our earliest experience of achieving balance — on the see-saw. In *Balancing Your Life* there is only one real difference from that childhood experience. Now, the person on the other end of the see-saw from you is *you*!

John Quinn
Producer/Presenter
RTÉ Radio

Introduction: About this Book

Have you ever asked yourself any of the following questions?

- Why do my children spend more time with minders than with me?

- Why am I spending every penny I earn?

- I'm close to the edge; how can I step back?

- I'm tired of walking a tightrope between my job and the rest of my life — is this what it's all about?

- What kind of society would we have if we weren't all so burnt out all the time?

If even one of these questions strikes a chord, then this book could be your lifeline. It doesn't matter who you are — whatever your age or background, whatever types of relationships you have, whether you are city- or country-based, whether or not you have children — you no doubt have one thing in common: you are managing and getting along from day to day, but you are also searching for a better quality of life.

What this Book Can Do for You

The message of this book is that a better quality of life *is* possible. More than that, happiness is possible. I believe that living a balanced life is central to happiness, and that examining our attitudes to time, work and money are steps on the road to balance. The book is not neutral on these subjects: I also believe that setting limits and deciding what is enough are crucial to the process. This entails challenging the contemporary myth that more is better. Most of us see through this myth already, but may not be clear where to go next, so the book can be a resource for identifying your next step. Many of the ideas in this book will be familiar, because I am drawing on philosophies and traditions from all over the world, ancient and contemporary. What is new is that it is written for an Irish context, using stories of people who have made changes in order to restore balance to their lives. It highlights a positive, alternative philosophy in an age of economic growth and increasingly harried everyday life.

My hope for the book is that it will be a guide to the choices open to you in trying to balance your life. It also aims to decrease the sense of isolation that many people feel in their search for balance and happiness. It encourages you to start with yourself, but also to work with other people in your search, and to see connections between your own lifestyle and national and global trends.

Although I attempt to practise a balanced lifestyle, I don't pretend to be an expert. For this reason, I consulted other people who have made a variety of choices for balance in their lives, and I discussed with them how and why they made these choices. Many of them discuss the issues in a much more eloquent fashion than I do. They are frank about the difficulties they experience, as well as the benefits of their choices. You might be inspired by their stories to take the next step towards fashioning the life you want.

The reflections, exercises and questions in this book are designed to demystify happiness and to help you make the transition from a fraught lifestyle to a more balanced one. These exercises show you that you can do it, but with the proviso that there are no blueprints — it is a matter of making the changes most appropriate to your personal circumstances. As Mark Burch writes, "finding a better way of life is a matter of degree, not of meeting an absolute standard".

Many citizens are so busy working and making a living that they have little time to stop and ponder the issues facing us in Ireland today, never mind take action to create the kind of society we would like to live in. There is very little writing available that gives practical suggestions about what type of action one can take (see Bibliography for some examples). This book does not claim to fill that gap completely, but it shows how we can at least create breathing space to start reflecting. It thus provides one link in the chain of resources to transform people from consumers — cogs in the wheel of an economy — into active citizens of a society.

Why I Wrote this Book

Part of my work involves interviewing people from a variety of backgrounds for social research, which over the years has given me valuable insights into other people's lives. It amazes me that so many people lead lives of quiet resignation, feeling that there is nothing they can do to be happy, that "reality" and "progress" mean making do with situations they don't particularly like. I got the idea for this book in late 1999, while I was researching for a report entitled *How Was It For You? Learning from couples' experiences in their first year of marriage.* All of the couples who participated were happy with their marriages. But many of them were dissatisfied with life. It would be wrong to describe them as very unhappy, but they felt that quality of life eluded them.

Time, paid work and money were the big issues in their lives. These people felt constantly tired and pressed for time. They complained that they didn't have enough time for each other, for their friends and families. They disliked the amount of time they spent commuting, often sitting in cars in traffic jams. Most worried about how they would fit children into their lives, or assumed that the only option available to them for childcare was paid professional care. They assumed there was no alternative to working more, buying more, borrowing more, and becoming more disillusioned. They tended to blame factors outside their control for the shape of their lives. Many of them looked to buying things like furniture, holidays, cars or clothes in order to compensate for their dissatisfaction. They also tried to make friends and family happy by buying expensive gifts.

Most earned good money, yet few had savings. They seemed mystified about where their money went, and they didn't keep records of their spending. They were trapped in a cycle of working, earning and spending most or all of what they earned. In several cases, they also worried about what might happen if they were made redundant from their jobs.

Several of the research participants felt that they could not keep going this way, yet they could see no alternative. They were so busy coping with working, commuting and simply surviving the rat race, that they had no time to take think creatively about alternatives.

For a couple of years before I did the research for *How Was It For You?* I had also been grappling with some of these issues in my own life (you can read my story in Chapter One). But what really set me on the road to writing this book was a second group of couples in the study. These couples had broken out of the work–earn–spend cycle and expressed satisfaction with their lives. They took responsibility for creating the quality of life they wanted, even if that meant having fewer material possessions and living on comparatively small incomes. They enjoyed modest houses, cars, furnishing and clothes. They resisted over-stretching themselves financially to take out a mortgage, even if the alternative was renting. They also avoided other forms of debt, such as car loans or credit card debt. Many of them had savings, however small, which provided a cushion for emergencies. The striking thing about them was that they had decided to prioritise happiness and wellbeing. In short, they were critical of consumerist values and believed that the most important things in life are relationships and time for friends, family, community and personal development. By having a vision of how they wanted their lives to be, and by developing financial intelligence, they had come to solutions that gave them sufficient money to live comfortably.

These "quality of life" couples were all very different from each other. A small number of couples already had children and some of these were quite traditional in their approach to gender roles, the women staying at home to care for children, while the men earned the incomes. In other cases, both partners cut back on paid work, so that they could both look after a baby. In the case of one couple who had no children, both partners worked part-time, and devoted time to voluntary work. But what they all had in common was that, rather than judging their lives by outward, easily measured standards of success, they judged them by qualitative standards which they set for themselves.

This book is not just for married people or couples or parents. The people who contributed to *How Was It For You?* were all quite young, married and Dublin-based. But they set me thinking. I decided to seek out more people who had taken the time to prioritise happiness and wellbeing. I wanted to find people who were single, married, at different life stages, with and without children, rural, provincial and urban-based. I wanted to put together some kind of guide, which would draw on the philosophy of *enough*, and which readers could use in making their own qualitative improvements relating to time, work, money and happiness.

Of course, there are people who are quite happy with the way things are. They have been able to buy second homes in Ireland and abroad, have three holidays a year, and the latest in kitchens, conservatories, clothing and cars. They enjoy good salaries, freedom of action and can jet to any place in the world that takes their fancy. Why should they change what already provides so much pleasure? If you are enjoying such affluence, you may not be quite as open to the message of *enough* that this book offers. Nevertheless, if you still feel that, despite your affluence, there is something missing, then the philosophy could have something for you too.

As we seek quality in our lives, it also becomes clear that none of our problems or choices exists in isolation. In learning to live wisely within ourselves, our families and our immediate communities, we are automatically drawn into the broader questions about a balanced future for Irish and global society. To comprehend the bigger picture, we need to use our mental "cameras" both to pull back and take wide shots and to zoom in and focus at all levels of society. So the book also takes some wide shots, which show how personal lifestyles fit into the bigger picture.

How to Use this Book

The book is not intended to provide a blueprint for balance, or a definitive list of "how to" techniques that you should follow in a prescribed order. The chapters are linked to each other, but it is not essential to read them in the order in which they are presented. And in many cases, it doesn't matter in what order you read the sections within the chapters — you can dip into them as it suits you. You might also find the index helpful.

Chapter One, *Change is Possible*, gives an overview of the concept of enough through history, and tells you something about my own journey. Chapter Two, *What Do You Want From Life?* begins with the premise that every practical action starts with a plan. It puts the philosophy of enough to work by helping you to draw up a life vision, so that you can decide what is a "good life" for you. Chapter Three, *Slowing the Treadmill of Work*, makes suggestions for getting your paid work under control, if you need to do so. Chapter Four, *Slowing the Treadmill Even More*, goes a step further in suggesting changes in your working life, while Chapter Five, *Work and Life*, examines attitudes and expectations concerning paid and unpaid work. Chapter Six, *Developing Financial Intelligence*, is concerned with our attitudes to money and its role in our lives, since money is a central issue for anybody who wants to balance their life today. Many of us have no financial focus, and this chapter has suggestions for developing one. Chapter Seven, *Out of the Rat Race and Into Life: Downshifters Tell their Stories*, provides pen pictures of five people who left stressful jobs and frenzied lifestyles, and are earning money from freelance work, but without over-extending themselves. Chapter Eight, *It's Not Just a Fad*, tells the stories of people who have been somewhat unconventional all their adult lives, and who have combined satisfying lifestyles and ways of earning money. They are long-timers in their search for balance, rather than recent refugees from the boom of the 1990s. Since early adulthood, they have been creative about living well, sometimes on very small incomes. Chapter Nine, *Live Well on Less Money*, continues to help you to explore the role of money in your life and in your search for balance, by providing practical suggestions for reducing your outgoings. Chapter Ten, *Using Time Wisely in Your Balanced Life,* outlines the ways that escaping the work–earn–spend cycle enhances health and happiness. It also explores issues concerning children and teenagers, and suggests ways to start learning groups. Chapter Eleven, *Final Thoughts: the Ideas, the People and the Bigger Picture,* draws together the book's themes, and encourages you to take your first steps if you have not already done so.

Each chapter can stand alone, so you can start wherever you find most appealing. You may like some chapters better than others. For instance, you may like to read all the case studies at once, and draw your own conclusions, or you may prefer to read the more practical chapters about work and money first. Alternatively, you may like to read the first and last chapters, which take a more general approach, before you read the practical suggestions or the case studies.

Having scanned the book, you may decide that its ideas are not for you just now. Change does not happen in the same way or at the same time for everybody. Why not set a time to come back to the book, and to review its ideas again? Wherever and whenever you start, and however you use it, this book recognises all its readers as people who can make changes happen, and who are capable of shaping balanced futures.

Chapter One

CHANGE IS POSSIBLE

Life in contemporary Ireland is a rat race for many people. The country has just come through a period of unprecedented economic growth, which has brought more spending power, more material possessions and more mobility than ever before. We are encouraged to believe that we can have it all. Yet, house prices are astronomical, people often have huge mortgages and live miles from their workplaces. Many spend hours commuting, much of that time at a standstill or a crawl in traffic. Some workers drive to their work location at 5.00 or 6.00 a.m., with children, duvets and breakfast in their cars. They arrive early enough to get a parking space, then go back to sleep and wait until the crèche opens.

Conventional and complementary health practitioners are seeing increasing numbers of patients whose sleeping patterns are disrupted by shift working and whose general health is also suffering as a consequence. Volunteering is declining, and calls to support groups such as Parentline are increasing. Vast housing estates are empty of people all day, and gated communities are becoming more common, because residents are increasingly worried about security. Savings are at an all-time low, especially among the under-35s, and credit card spending and personal debt are at an all-time high.

Many experience life as intrinsically meaningless. Loneliness is common, even in crowded shopping malls. More and more people are indulging in "retail therapy", drugs and alcohol in order to compensate for the meaningless nature of their lives. Suicide is on the increase and although it is impossible to know the causes in every case, it is safe to assume that at least some arise from a lack of connectedness to the social fabric. Our connections with other people too often rely on having money that can pay for services or demonstrate status.

In this context, it is tempting to think that change is impossible. Most people, when questioned, say that happiness and peace of mind are their priorities, and they assert that money cannot buy them, after a certain level of material need is provided for. But because the problems seem overwhelming, people tend to assume that they need to make extreme moves, in order to create happier lives. They see a mountain instead of a series of small, easily scalable peaks. Indeed, in spite of the common assertion that money cannot buy happiness, many live in hope of a lottery win or some other windfall, and are unaware of what they can do here and now.

Small is Significant

Small changes can be very significant, however. One does not have to drop out, or appear different, in order to make qualitative changes in one's life. You can reduce your bills, examine your possessions and how they serve you, and get rid of excess. You can also consider options like working four days a week instead of five, working from home and saving on commuting time, or building a portfolio of different jobs, possibly freelance, but avoiding overload. Dual-income couples may decide to live on one full-time or two part-time incomes and some households may get rid of a second car. Other people choose not to own a car; they walk, cycle or use public transport, perhaps hiring a car when they need one.

Living a balanced life, or making changes towards a balanced life, can take the simple form of becoming aware of, and challenging, commonly accepted attitudes to paid work, possessions and success. These attitudes include: more is better; faster is better; success is rising up a career ladder; promotion is more important than staying in a job you enjoy; and the customer or job deserves priority always. The book encourages you to examine where and how these attitudes are affecting your life, and to consider where and how you might make changes. It offers you guidelines for examining the benefits and downsides of making such changes, and for deciding the most suitable steps for you. Money and work are central to all of these steps, so a large proportion of the book is devoted to examining our attitudes to them and the sources of these attitudes, as well as the alternatives that we can embrace.

This trend towards scaling back on paid work, reducing expenses and spending less is known as *downshifting*, and a lot has been written about it in Britain, the USA and Canada, although it has not received much media attention in Ireland until recently. It revolves around the concept of knowing what is *enough* to ensure quality in every area of one's life, and it is in direct contrast to the philosophy of having it all. Many self-help books emphasise saying yes to everything, but this one emphasises the importance of saying no. This takes courage, but it is very manageable if you take it slowly, choosing carefully where to start. In your search for balance, I encourage you to downshift in many ways. But in very tangible ways, downshifting is upgrading the quality of life.

It has become a cliché to say that Ireland and the Irish are at a point where we can choose what sort of a future we want. But many citizens feel unable to make choices for themselves, and rely on government or employers to initiate change that will enhance quality of life. This feeling of lack of control came across very strongly among the dissatisfied couples in my study *How Was It For You?* It was striking that the dissatisfied participants blamed outside forces. They constantly asserted that "they", that is, somebody else, should do something about their problems. They lacked the ability to see that they could actually take the initiative, following the advice of Mahatma Gandhi, who said that "you must be the change you wish to see in the world".

I am not suggesting that government and other official policies are not important, or that individuals acting alone can change society. Your efforts to live a balanced life are not going to alleviate social problems overnight. But a sea change in the ways that individuals live could have gradual effects towards creating communities that prioritise quality of life, and wellbeing on a greater scale. So I am suggesting that, as individuals, we should not wait around for somebody else to do something, but that we can take the first steps, communicate with other people about why we are taking them, and ultimately work with others to create a new culture where citizens and government together improve quality of life. You don't have to wait for society to change first — you can be one of those who initiates the change.

Yet we are all ambivalent about change. The will to change exists alongside the desire to remain the same, and for good reason, as Magda Goldhor Lerner points out. Change is risky and unknown — sameness is reassuring and predictable, even if laden with dissatisfaction. Sometimes we are forced to change our attitudes and our behaviours concerning work, money and time, because of illness, bereavement, a mid-life review or redundancy. Other times, we choose change in a planned way. Balancing your life is not a simple task, because the world is complex. You will make mistakes along the way, because you are doing something you have never done before. But you can learn from your mistakes, and this book is about encouraging you on your journey.

Balance throughout History

The idea of balancing one's life may seem to have a particular relevance in the contemporary world, but the desire for a balanced life is not new, and many traditions and philosophies promote the concept of enough as a means to balance and happiness. The concept is expressed in terms such as simplicity, frugality, moderation, appreciation of nature, a critique of materialism, anti-consumerism, and mindfulness.

In the Western world, the roots of the concept go back at least to the Ancient Greeks and the notion of the "golden mean". Early and medieval Christianity also promoted a philosophy of sufficiency. The Bible refers frequently to the need to balance material and spiritual aspects of life, illustrated in the line "Give me neither poverty nor wealth", from Proverbs 30:8. Francis of Assisi embraced poverty, giving away his father's money following illness. The Celtic Christian tradition of Columba, Brigid and Patrick also promoted frugal living.

In the first half of the eighteenth century, Amish communities established themselves across the United States, practising both pacifism and communism. They still live today without many of the "necessities" of contemporary society, such as cars, tractors or telephones, and they promote the value and dignity of work that is concerned with essential tasks.

In nineteenth-century America, the transcendentalist Henry Thoreau lived in the New England countryside, documenting the relationship between people and nature. His writings and those of Ralph Waldo Emerson helped to promote a simple-living aesthetic that had been established with the arrival of the Pilgrim Fathers from England. Slightly later, in Russia, Leo Tolstoy promoted the same ideal of simple living. Tolstoy corresponded with Mahatma Gandhi, and was directly influenced by his thought.

In Victorian England, William Morris and the Arts and Crafts Movement opposed the effects of the Industrial Revolution, which made work into something separate from the rest of life, and divorced people from the rhythms of the natural world, the seasons and communities.

For thousands of years in the East, the spiritual traditions of Buddhism, Hinduism, Taoism and Jainism have also promoted the virtues of moderation, mindfulness and spirituality as a way to enlightenment. Taoism promotes the idea that less is actually more. Buddhism recognises that material needs must be met, and teaches the practice of a middle way between deprivation and material extravagance.

Mahatma Gandhi, one of the greatest Indian teachers, opposed materialism and believed in the deliberate and voluntary reduction of wants. He practised frugality in his daily life, and wrote that Europeans were in danger of becoming enslaved to the material comforts to which they were accustomed.

Returning to Western society, in the late nineteenth century, the American sociologist Thorstein Veblen coined the term "conspicuous consumption", defining it as the means by which the new rich could establish their status, in the absence of inherited status. The phenomenon of consumerism had come under scrutiny.

In the 1970s, those who rejected consumerism in the West were largely characterised as dropouts. Many went back to the land, aiming for self-sufficiency. Concerns about ecological damage and the environment encouraged the promotion of an alternative set of values by which to live. E.F. Schumacher's book, *Small is Beautiful*, applied the Buddhist middle way to economics, describing the ideal economy as one that provides an adequate range of material goods and whose production processes are in harmony with the environment and with available resources.

In the early 1980s, the American Duane Elgin popularised the term "voluntary simplicity", which was based of the teachings of Gandhi. Elgin used it to describe lifestyle choices that could be both rewarding and sustainable. Its tenets were frugal consumption, ecological awareness and personal development. Elgin was clear that his message was one of balance, not poverty, and empowerment, not self-denial.

In 1992, Vicki Robin and Joe Dominguez published *Your Money or Your Life*, asserting that the key to a richer, more meaningful existence was re-negotiating one's relationship with money and reaching an understanding of enough. They put forward a nine-step plan for eliminating personal debt, achieving what they call financial intelligence and improving the quality of life. This practical work, which was nevertheless rooted in a very strong critique of consumerism, became a bestseller in the United States and has also sold well in several translations.

Sustainability and Downshifting

In recent decades, much of the thinking about enough has come under the banner of *sustainability*. Theory and practice concerning the economics of sustainability and sustainable development have given us ways to think about the proper limits to economic development, limits to the demands we make on the environment and the planet as a whole, and limits to the stresses we place on the fabric of social life. The economist Herman Daly urges us to take very seriously the idea of when to stop. Sustainability, then, is seen as a way to live comfortably within the confines of one's economic, social and environmental limits, and to build satisfying community life. It is considered essential to the pursuit of equality, social justice and a good quality of life for everybody on the planet.

The global issues concerning sustainability are part of what this book examines, but mostly it deals with the problems and solutions in relation to the quality of personal lives. In America, and later, in Britain, the term "downshifting" gradually gained currency as a way of describing a less-is-more approach to a good quality of life. Juliet Schor, a sociologist, has researched the extent of the phenomenon in the US, finding that it is a minority interest, but significant nonetheless. In Britain, the Henley Centre for Forecasting has also identified it as a significant concern for many Britons.

It is difficult to know how many people in Ireland see themselves as part of this trend. Even some of the people interviewed for this book don't use the term downshifting to describe themselves, some because they have never joined the conventional rat race and never been "up", in the words of one interviewee, and others because the term is not widely recognised. Most don't refer to a formal philosophy of enough, although it comes through in their stories and the ways they arrange their lives.

There are encouraging signs, however, of a growing recognition that we need more than material possessions and high incomes to bring about happiness. The culture of long working hours is identified as detrimental to individuals, families, relationships and communities, as well as to productivity and efficiency in business. Many community development groups and some political parties are taking sustainable development issues seriously. The Céifin Institute's conferences and publications on balance, sustainability and citizenship in the new millennium draw strong interest. Interest is also increasing in the work of the Sustainable Ireland Co-operative and in Feasta, The Foundation for the Economics of Sustainable Development. These initiatives are looking for ways forward in a time when Ireland is at risk of furthering economic growth at the expense of human and social development, along with equality and justice.

The Culturally Creative Approach to Balance

The philosophy of enough has honourable traditions. But in today's complex world, it is wise to scrutinise all traditions, taking into account what social movements for equality and social justice have taught us. Paul Ray and Sherry Anderson, authors of *The Cultural Creatives*, have identified three groups in the Western world: traditionals, moderns and cultural creatives. I suggest that in the search for balance, both personal and social, we need to question both tradition and modernity, as the cultural creatives do. Ray and Anderson's model looks something like the following.

The *moderns* are the largest cultural group. They operate with the assumption that economic growth is an unquestioned good, and actively prize materialism and the drive to acquire money and property. They tend to spend beyond their means, they take a cynical view of idealism, caring work, unpaid work, and those who define success in terms not related to money and status. They see the commercialised urban-industrialised world as the obvious right way to live, and think that the way to get on is to adapt to it. Moderns like to quantify things, and to measure them in numerical or monetary terms. They tend to see the body as a machine and the earth as a resource at the disposal of humans. They tend to believe that the way to remain in control of one's life is to compartmentalise it into discrete separate spheres, such as work, family, socialising, sex, education and politics. They tend to be dismissive of spirituality or personal development. Moderns tend to see gender equality as women's full-time participation in the paid labour force, and the taking on by women of roles traditionally associated with men. They believe in meritocracy, that is, that if you have talent and work hard, you will be rewarded with material success. "Having it all" is often the motto of the moderns.

However, for many moderns, paid work dominates to the extent that there is little time for self, family, community or for simply doing nothing. This situation is seen as the consequence of progress; it is considered that the old days are gone forever, and that it is naïve to believe that we can escape the general trends. Moderns reward themselves with weekend breaks, frequent holidays, meals out, shopping, massage and other therapy, new clothes, trips to the garden centre or DIY shop, drugs, and alcohol. Then they get back on the treadmill again. Many claim that there is no alternative, that the trappings of contemporary life are necessary and costly, so that they cannot even consider cutting back on paid work and earning less.

Many moderns deny what their lifestyles are doing to their emotional wellbeing. They tend to rely on technology to fix personal problems, or to buy satisfaction and wellbeing by means of material possessions and by experiences such as holidays, adventure and travel. These approaches often work in the short term, but tend to lose their appeal, or else to require that we spend increasing amounts of money on goods and services. Ironically, a culture of consumption does not provide the satisfaction and comfort that it promises. Therefore, many who subscribe to the modernist worldview are cynical about the meaning of life, and the possibilities for equality, justice and happiness on both local and global scales. Individualism and looking out for oneself become the norm. Discussing the changes in the Irish psyche which have come about in the past decade, Michael O'Connell characterises them as "brutal modernisation, with rampant consumerism and individualism leading the charge".

Traditionals, on the other hand, want to return to traditional ways of life and traditional gender roles. They tend towards religious conservatism and fundamentalism. They have images of happy communities in past times, where everybody shared beliefs, principles and values, usually underpinned by religion. They tend to gloss over the aspects of such communities that were oppressive: namely, the low status of women and children, the regulation of sexuality, the largely authoritarian nature of the church and education, and the closed nature of communities, with their suspicions of outsiders or difference.

Traditionals also believe in the value of caring work, volunteering, and working to create a better society. But because the past is a golden era for many traditionals, they see a return to it as the best option for improving quality of life. They tend to be very critical of moderns. Feminism and the challenging of gender roles are usually anathema to them. They are often suspicious of immigrants, fearing that they will destroy traditional ways of life and values. Moderns, on the other hand, tend to see traditionals as backward and outmoded.

Cultural creatives question both traditionalism and modernism, while not losing sight of what each of those worldviews has contributed to human development. For example, they understand the value of women's participation in the paid labour force, and its contribution to gender equality, but are critical of the way that this has contributed to the devaluation of unpaid caring work. They recognise the value of volunteering and caring and working to help others, as put forward by traditionals, but are critical of the rigidity of thinking that sees caring and other unpaid domestic work as primarily the responsibility of women. They put forward new ways of living that often come out of the same roots as many of the best traditions, such as care for children, community and spirituality, but they give a different expression to these, drawing on social movements such as feminism, environmentalism and anti-racism. They are aware of the complexity of contemporary social, political and economic issues, and of the need to avoid simplistic responses.

Cultural creatives value personal relationships, personal development, the environment, unpaid work, equality, quality of life, holistic approaches to health, learning about other cultures, spirituality and community. They are critical of consumerism, a "having it all" or "more is better" philosophy, debt and exploitation of the earth's peoples and resources. As with the people you will meet in this book, not all cultural creatives share exactly the same concerns, but they tend to be people whose approaches to life are complemented by a philosophy of enough. Most importantly, they believe in acting according to their values.

Some Irish people are living their own versions of cultural creativity, although we don't know how many. While it would be very instructive to do a nationwide survey, the stories you will read here were not collected by means of any statistical sampling. They "snowballed" as the research progressed during 2001 and 2002, and are snapshots of the lives of a small group of people in that period. But while the group I met is small, the values and principles that guide their lives are strong, and they resonate with many other people who are seeking quality of life.

Finding Enough in My Own Life

My own story has a part to play in the writing of this book. I consider myself a modest downshifter. I started my working life in 1979 as a vocational teacher. I enjoyed teaching, extra-curricular activities at weekends and my eventual job as a home-school links teacher. I always put a lot of effort into my job, and also took several courses and spent a lot of time studying. By the end of the 1990s, my life consisted of a routine of work, study and little else except keeping physically fit, although I always took six to eight weeks of a summer holiday.

In 1995, I decided to take a year's unpaid study leave, in order to work full-time on a doctoral thesis. Supported by my husband, Frank, who had a full-time teaching job, I studied for six months, with no income of my own. I then took on some part-time teaching and research work. Between the paid work and working on the thesis, I had very little free time. Work became my whole life. I loved my studies and the ideas I was developing, but often, I thought that there must be a better way to live. However, there seemed to be no way out of the route I was on. I imagined that when the thesis was finished, things would be better.

Although I was still working very hard, I wasn't earning a lot. One of the benefits of this situation was that I began to realise that we could live on a lot less money than we had imagined. When we had had two full salaries, our finances were often badly organised. Now, we scrupulously avoided overdraft and other debt. During the school year 1997–98, Frank took a year's unpaid leave and we were able to live on my earnings, which were still less than my potential earnings in my whole-time teaching job.

In 1998, when I was forty, I was awarded my doctorate. I knew that I would not go back to my school teaching job, so I resigned the post, even though I had the option of applying for further leave in the form of a career break. By this time, I had a full portfolio of work, made up of short-term research contracts and part-time teaching hours at the National University of Ireland, Maynooth. The university is about four miles from my home, and one of the attractions of working there was that I could cycle or use public transport, avoiding a long commute each day, in an increasingly congested greater Dublin area. Around this time, I began to think increasingly in terms of quality of life. I also began to stop worrying too much, although not completely, about the uncertainty surrounding my work — every time I finished one contract or project, another appeared. Frank went back to his job, but on a job-sharing basis for two years.

When I started to study for the PhD, it was because I loved the ideas I was working with and the research I was doing. I naïvely believed that the qualification was an end point, only to later realise that, in the university system, it is only the beginning. One's worth is judged on the number and type of publications produced each year. For a while, I applied for academic posts in different universities and knew that I needed to have a publications record in order to be considered for them. I also put some pressure on myself to publish — I wanted to have my ideas circulated and discussed, and to establish a scholarly reputation for myself. In short, I was on the verge of becoming involved in the academic treadmill of writing and publishing, and fitting those activities in around teaching and administration.

My work life was uncertain and demanding and I was often exhausted. But it also had its advantages: I did not work for a boss in the conventional way, but decided what projects to become involved in; I was able to avoid contracts that involved working in the summer. I was working close to home, and I was doing work that for the most part I enjoyed and was good at. I knew that I hadn't got the balance quite right, and that I had to tackle the issue of overwork, but I felt that I was on the right road.

One of the issues that caused me most annoyance was part-time teaching. In the university system, a part-time lecturer gets paid for hours in the classroom only. Preparation time is unpaid. Often, I spent four or more hours preparing a lecture, then an hour delivering it, for a gross payment of £40 (about €50), at that time. More often than not, these lectures took place at night (with part-time students who attended in the evenings), so by the time I was going home, a take-away or a drink seemed attractive, putting an immediate hole in my pay. Preparing the lectures also took time from the better-paid research work and from my own writing, and meant that I spent extra time at my desk. Stiff shoulders and neck often brought me to a massage therapist, because I didn't always make time to do my exercises and stretching.

Another problem I experienced was a lack of time. We have no children, but I still didn't seem to have enough time to see friends regularly, to cook for friends, look after our garden, or to see family members as often as I would have liked. Although I have always eaten healthy food and stayed fit, I felt tired most of the time.

At the point when these issues were really beginning to exasperate me, I read in Joe Armstrong's *Irish Times* column about the book *Your Money or Your Life,* by Vicki Robin and Joe Dominguez. Armstrong mentioned their method of calculating the costs of a job, and whether the payment was worth the effort and costs combined. This idea alone was enough to prompt me to buy the book, which is a tool for re-evaluating attitudes to work, money and life in general. It is a radical book, to which I refer again many times in this book. But just two of its ideas helped me get things in perspective.

The first idea is that one should calculate all the costs associated with a job — the actual amount of time spent, the dress costs, commuting costs, costs in terms of stress — and take them into account in calculating the real hourly return for a job. Related to this concept is the idea that one should charge as much for one's time as is consistent with one's health and integrity. Using these criteria, one can decide if particular jobs are worth taking on. This new way of thinking allowed me to decide that I was no longer prepared to teach on a pay-by-the hour basis, since the amount of money in my pay cheque did not reflect the amount of effort involved. It may seem obvious to many readers, but what it did for me was to give me tools to be assertive enough to say "no" to this way of working. Teaching was one of the activities that I found most tiring, even though I enjoyed it. The benefits were outweighed by the disadvantages, and that made teaching an activity with a very poor return. Once I had the concepts to examine my paid work in this way, I was able to articulate what it was about teaching that made it not worth my while. Following that, I was able to decide to cut it back drastically.

The second concept that was hugely important to me was the idea that we need to decide what is enough for us, in terms of possessions, money, personal and professional achievement. This concept challenges the notion that aspirations need to be constantly expanding. Of course, having met this concept in *Your Money or Your Life*, I started meeting it in lots of places. Charles Handy, for example, contends that the first step towards personal freedom is deciding what is enough. The concept recurs throughout this book. In relation to my personal story, however, it marked a crucial change in the way I viewed my paid work and my fledgling academic career.

As I reviewed my career, I had to ask what I really wanted from my studies and all the effort I had made. Did I want to spend all my non-paid working time writing for scholarly journals, in order to build a CV that might eventually lead to a full-time academic post? Or should I prioritise my health, happiness, relationships and personal development, while still doing a modest amount of writing — enough writing — about my academic ideas? As I read in a more organised fashion about balanced living, I realised that I knew a lot of people who have been quietly, undramatically, but nevertheless significantly, doing just that, for years. It was only latterly that I realised what they were doing.

Currently, I have stopped applying for jobs — I earn money from a portfolio of freelance research, writing, group facilitation and a small number of teaching hours. I have a base at the Centre for Adult and Community Education at NUI Maynooth, which gives me the benefits of supportive colleagues, while allowing the Centre to benefit from my research, writing and ideas. Although I'm not sure how long this arrangement will continue, I also have faith that I will continue to find convivial work. I'm building the confidence to charge a realistic rate for the work I do. I also occasionally turn work away, either because it does not interest me, or because I have too many projects on the go. I am able to work flexibly, often at times to suit myself, and quite often from home. Each summer, I take at least two months without any paid work. I have decided not to get over-involved in academic publishing, but to write occasional articles, which I can manage in the time available to me, while allowing me to pursue the ideas I care about.

In our household, we continue to monitor where every penny goes, so that we can analyse our spending habits and see where we can make savings. We still have a mortgage, but avoid other debt. I earn just over half of what I would earn if I had remained in my teaching job. We are careful about where and how we spend our money, but our finances have never been in better shape, and we consider that we live very well and have everything we want.

I am not a perfectly balanced individual. I have times of uncertainty and frustration. I still need to pay attention to my tendency to overwork, a tendency to be a perfectionist, and a difficulty with saying no. I understand that balance is a process, rather than a place, and this understanding is reflected in this book also. But I am happier than I have ever been, working and living as I do now. Most of all, I value the freedom I have gained from working with a concept of enough.

Happiness Doesn't Just Happen

In *Flow: The Psychology of Happiness*, Mihaly Csikszentmihalyi writes that happiness is a condition that must be prepared for and cultivated. You have to be proactive about it. Happiness is often portrayed in consumer society as "having it all", meaning that we ought not to experience any limitations. But having it all tends to make us focused on external signs of success, and is not based on a personal vision of one's values and purposes in life. Happiness is both inner- and outer-directed. It demands a high degree of self-knowledge, an ability to create one's own meanings, along with self-assertion, while at the same time it demands engagement with the outer world and integration with other people.

You will realise by now that this book takes a particular stance on the subject of happiness. It asserts that happiness comes from knowing what is enough for our needs. It encourages us to draw up our own definitions of success, excellence and achievement, which are connected to understanding our limits and our life purpose. The philosophy of enough demands an active engagement with life. It takes courage to say "no" to the "more is better" culture in which we live, and to live within one's own limits. But *enough* is a powerful position to adopt, and a liberating philosophy. It fosters a sense of meaning and of confidence in oneself, which are also strongly connected with happiness.

Learning to understand what is enough for oneself develops a sense of security. While the future cannot be predicted, one can feel confident about being able to deal with its complexities and ambiguities, by taking responsibility for how one responds to it. Taking responsibility like this is a type of power very different from the power and status that material wealth can provide, which are no guarantee of happiness.

Anyone in contemporary Ireland who writes about happiness founded in a philosophy of enough risks being branded naïve. The philosophy of enough challenges at least two different approaches to happiness current in today's cynical culture: that happiness can be bought; and that happiness is not possible. While it challenges those beliefs, the book does not see happiness as a simple end point or a state that we can reach if we follow certain steps. Robert E. Lane points out that happiness involves being able to give maximum attention to the things that are most important to you. A balanced life won't protect you from illness, accidents, difficult decisions, problems with children, colleagues or neighbours, or from worries about parents, friends and siblings. But it will provide the conditions whereby you can give the attention you deem appropriate to those issues, if and when they arise. Happiness is not about opting out or disconnecting from society in any way, but it comes about as a spin-off from a life of engagement.

Chapter Two

WHAT DO YOU WANT FROM LIFE?

To find fulfilment, you need to know what you are looking for. You need to constantly ask yourself, "Why am I doing what I'm doing?" You need to have your own definitions of a successful life. Only then will you know when you have arrived at enough for you. Neither our educational system nor TV and other media encourage us to develop inspirational plans for our lives. We are encouraged to think in fairly short-term ways about what we want from life. It is not part of popular culture to dwell on the things that we value in the overall picture of our lives.

"Visions alone don't produce results, but we'll never produce results without them," writes Donella Meadows. Stephen Covey suggests that all things are created twice. You begin with a vision, where you imagine and plan. This is the first, mental, creation — the script. The second creation is physical — how you actually carry out the plan that takes you towards your vision. Most of us live according to the script that is most common in our time. But balancing your life demands creating a vision that is your own. Then, as you live each day of this life, you remind yourself of what your end result should look like. You begin, as Covey puts it, with the end in mind. Whatever stage of our lives we are at, it is always possible to look within, to visualise what is possible for us, and to figure out ways to make it a reality.

Thinking about Enough as the Basis for a Life Vision

Balancing your life means a wise use of money, time, energy and possessions — getting all of them just right, so that you have enough of everything, without personal or planetary waste. *Enough* is not about being a skinflint or living with low standards, but about appreciating everything to its maximum, being able to get pleasure from small things and everyday events, as well as big events and special occasions. Growth, in a context of enough, means quality rather than quantity. Pursuing the good life by means of money, career or possessions takes an enormous amount of energy. We always want more and we never know when we have arrived. The concept of enough is the opposite of that.

Enough encourages you to think about limits. It teaches you to adjust your expectations of yourself. It deconstructs advertising and the ways it tries to construct desires and identities, continually moving the goalposts and raising the so-called standards, so that we become confused about what our needs are. Don't believe the advertising that tells you it is appropriate to always want more. Your ambitions need to be "decently modest", in the words of Charles Handy. Your achievements don't have to be earth-shattering, as long as they are meaningful to you. Enough helps you to let go and to say "no". You need to understand enough, in order to decide when an activity, a way of life, a type of work, an ambition, a standard, or a certain role is no longer providing fulfilment. Then you can let it go and explore other choices. This demands a high degree of self-knowledge.

Enough also teaches you to reduce the expectations you have of partners, children, friends and associates. We need to set limits here too. In intimate relationships, we have allowed expectations of what another person can do for us to become inflated. We tend to place extraordinary demands on a partner to make us happy and meet our needs. In fact, the only person you should rightly have expectations of is yourself. You are the only person whose actions you can control, but by making personal changes, you can change the dynamics of relationships for the better.

In the business world, unrealistically high expectations can lead us to be impatient with other people, to treat them with contempt if service is not up to our expectations, to forget that they are human and make mistakes. When we understand the concept of limits in ourselves and are putting them into practice, so that we are not rushed or overextended, then there is more time to allow for other people's humanness. We take responsibility for our part of the encounter. Similarly, we learn not to place too much blame on government or leaders for the state of our society. We avoid the assertion that "they should do something about it". We take responsibility for our own roles in the creation of the social fabric. We can all become leaders, questioning the taken-for-granted, and developing new ways of living and working.

Taking Stock

The first step on the road is to stop and think about what you are doing now. What do you like about your lifestyle and what are you dissatisfied with? What aspects of time, work, money and relationships are you happy with? Where would you like to make changes? What do the activities that take up most of your time express about you? How would someone who could see only the external things about you describe you? What values, purpose and dreams would they ascribe to you? Would they see your true values, purposes and dreams, or a way of life devoted to working towards someone else's ends? It is worth devoting time to these and similar questions as a way of taking stock.

Alternatively, imagine yourself dying tomorrow. Where will your thoughts be? Will you wish you had earned more money, or that you had more to leave in your estate? Will you wish you had worn more stylish clothing during your lifetime, or had nicer haircuts, or a more toned body, or that you impressed lots of people with the cars you drove, or the houses you lived in, or the holidays you took? Will you wish that you had been more powerful, or that you had had more pleasure?

"My deepest belief is that to live as if we're dying can set us free," writes Anne Lamott. As you come to the end of your life, it's far more likely that you will bring your attention to the people in your life and the relationships you have had, any worthwhile work you have accomplished, and memories of friends and family, rather than things like money, power, possessions or appearance. Thinking of our dying can provide clarity about what we value in the present. The next section also shows how thinking about our own death can help to clarify our vision of life.

Having thought about some of the topics above, how do you see your life? What is good about it and what is missing? Did the questions challenge any of your beliefs about yourself? What are your relationships like? What are you willing to admit to yourself about your situation, without judging rights and wrongs? Do you want to continue your present lifestyle? Be gentle with yourself as you ponder these questions. The philosophy of enough is a gentle one, and the questions are not a suggestion that a person should be judged solely according to external criteria. They are about reflecting on memories, events and experiences that have given us inner joy and a sense of fulfilment, and finding ways to increase these in our lives. But the questions do imply that we can make choices about how to live, choices which reflect our values.

Sadly, many people are involved in ways of life that they didn't really choose and that have come to feel like traps. To get out of these traps, we need to realise where we are in the first place. To use an image from Stephen Covey, we can be very busy, working incredibly hard climbing, or just trying to stay on, a metaphorical ladder, only to find, when we stop and think, that the ladder is up against the wrong wall. Or we may never stop to think at all, until we have used all our energy in climbing the ladder. Then, when we get to the top, we may see that it has brought us to a place where we may not want to be. You need to get a clear picture of the wall where you would like to place your ladder. Equally important, you need to know where you don't want to put it. Behind every decision about where to place the ladder, that is, a decision to shape a future, there is a vision of what a life should look like.

Starting out with the End in Mind

In order to create a vision, several writers, including Stephen Covey and Charles Handy, suggest that you imagine the funeral or memorial service that you would really like for yourself. If you have never done this or a similar exercise, it is worth a try, as it can be very effective in putting us in touch with what we really want from life. Imagine what you would like significant people to say about you. Choose five people to speak: someone from among your family, your friends, your work associates, your local community and your community of interest. What kind of spouse, parent, sibling, son, daughter or cousin would you like to hear described by your family member? What would you like your friend, your colleague and the community member to say? What would you like them to remember about you? What kind of relationships and achievements would you like them to report?

- Take some quiet time to do this visualisation exercise. If you take it seriously, it will put you in touch with some of the most important things in your life.

- Make some notes about the experience.

- What differences do you note between what you would like to be remembered for, and the things you think people would *actually* think and say, at least privately, if you died tomorrow?

- How can you get to the point where the speakers at your real memorial service will say the kinds of things you would like to hear?

These activities are not about being remembered as a high achiever, in the usual sense of that phrase. They are not about appearances and external indicators of conventional success, but are a way of reflecting on what a good enough life might be for you.

You don't have to do this all at once. Organise the time for it in the way that suits you. But do it, or something like it. Charles Handy says that he has stopped doing it in this way in latter years, but every year writes letters to his children, to be read by them when he is gone, in which he tries to spell out the values which guide his life. If these thoughts of death are not for you, you could try Dave Ellis's book, *Shaping Your Future: Five steps to the life of your dreams.*

What's Stopping You Developing a Vision?

Sometimes, awareness and an appreciation of your connections to what is around you are all you need as the first step in thinking about your vision. If you can look beyond the taken-for-granted and the common-sense understanding of "the way things are", you have a head start. Maybe, though, you just can't get started. Below, I consider some of the reasons why this might be so. None of the barriers to vision is insurmountable.

Cynicism

You cannot begin to muse on the vision of a successful life if you are cynical. Cynicism is a destructive state of mind that negates the value of everything. Scepticism, on the other hand, is necessary. It involves the healthy questioning of taken-for-granted truths, the questioning of authority, convention and common sense. You are going to need it in large quantities if you are going to balance your life in today's world. But you do not need cynicism.

Blaming Others

Conventional ways of thinking encourage us to blame others for our unsatisfactory experiences. Very often, though, we have many more options open to us than we realise. Stop blaming, and start taking responsibility. This is the first step towards freedom. If you exercise even the tiniest bit of responsibility, in even the most seemingly inconsequential part of your life, your freedom will grow.

If you think that's all very well for some, but that some people have absolutely no choices, remind yourself that you are an adult, and read Viktor Frankl's book, *Man's Search for Meaning*. Frankl, an Austrian Jew, was incarcerated in concentration camps during the Second World War. Based on his experiences, he believed that humans could always choose their attitude, even in the worst of circumstances.

Inability to focus on anything good in your current lifestyle

You can't always have everything you want, right now. So you need to focus on what is good about your present life. Creating a vision is not about what you would do with all the money if you won the lotto. It's more like imagining what it is in your life now that contains the seeds of all the things you would like to do. If you find that you are living constantly in "if only" mode, or concentrating on what is wrong in your life, you should first discover what is positive and within your control. Learn to enjoy those things, even to increase them. Then you will have something on which to base your vision.

Serious personal problems

If you have a major personal difficulty, such debt, or a psychological or emotional block of some kind, or severe depression, it may be very difficult to get beyond it, in order to do any kind of vision exercises. If you need help with something like this, seek it in a supportive environment. Debt counselling is available free from the Money Advice and Budgeting Service (MABS), and Chapters Six and Nine, which deal with money issues, will also be useful. A trustworthy therapist or spiritual advisor will be able to put you on the road to dealing with psychological or emotional difficulties. There's no need to abandon the idea of creating a vision, but it may be easier to start somewhere else.

If you suffer from mild chronic depression, however, don't use it as an excuse not to get started. This kind of depression can manifest itself as fatigue, boredom, or lack of enthusiasm, and the World Health Organisation predicts that by 2010 it will be the second commonest disease in the developed world. Your depression may actually be giving you a message that you need to start looking for meaning in your life, and working on a vision is a way to do this.

Other people's visions

Many of our current visions come from advertising images, on both radio and TV. In most Western European countries, the average person watches three to four hours TV per day. The intent of advertising is to get us to see life as a non-stop stream of commodities. Buy something, do something; commodities are life. But these are visions created by other people, rather than by ourselves, in order to make us consume more.

Another powerful creator of our visions is exposure to what our friends, family and work associates do and have. Often, we do things because it's what everybody else does. This is ironic in a multicultural, multimedia society, where so much emphasis is placed on consumer choice and individuality. Over-reliance on other people's visions prevents us from recognising what we need for fulfilment. We tend to lose touch with our own imaginations and the ability to create our own visions. In the long run, this means that we spend our time, money and energy aspiring to goals that we did not create for ourselves. Moderate or eliminate your exposure to TV and commercial radio, and be wary of trying to have and do the same things as people around you.

Not enough time

Sometimes we are so busy working and just surviving that we cannot take the time to think and plan. A holiday can be a good time to review your situation. If you have one coming up, why not equip yourself with pen and paper and set aside some time for reflection? Or you could consider taking a week off, specifically for the purpose of developing a vision. Even better, think of a career break or sabbatical. If you can't do any of those things, use the ideas in Chapter Three for making work more manageable, and thus creating more time in your life in general.

Doing More Work on Your Vision

Use the notes you made from visualising your memorial or funeral service to make some further notes in answer to the questions below.

What roles do you occupy?

Our roles arise because of our connections and responsibilities to other people or to our work. It is healthy to experience a number of roles, but some of us experience role overload, where we have many roles and not enough time to attend to each one as we would like. There is also a danger in having to switch between roles a number of times a day — it can disorienting, unbalancing, and difficult to focus fully on each. Others have few roles. Those who achieve very highly, in the conventional sense of achievement, often occupy a very limited number of roles. It is always easier to achieve in one sphere if you don't have to take responsibility in others.

- List your various roles. Think about who needs you, and the people you need in your life.
- How did you come to occupy each role?
- What demands does each one make?
- What rewards does each one offer?
- How do you measure success or achievement in each role?
- Rank them in order of importance.
- Which roles would you like to develop? How can you do this?
- Which new roles would you like to take on? How can you do this?
- Are there some you would like to give up or reduce? How can you do this? What would the consequences be?

What are your values?

Values are the ideals and beliefs on which we base our decisions to live and act in certain ways. They guide our sense of right and wrong. How we spend our time and our money reflects our values. How we choose to relate to other people does too, as do the emotions we feel. What we consider essential in our lives also reflects our values.

- Make a list of the values you can identify from your vision exercise. List as many as you can.

- With whom do you share these values?

- Which values are clear from your current lifestyle?

- Are you prevented from acting on some of your values? How? Why? How could this be different?

What are your dreams?

Make a list of the dreams you have got in touch with, as a result of your vision exercise. They might be old dreams re-activated, or new ones. List them all, without exception. You could use some of the questions below to help you.

- What dreams have you achieved? Was the effort worth it?

- What dreams are you in the process of achieving?

- Do you think it's too late for you to achieve some of your dreams? Why?

- What have you long wanted to do, that you haven't done yet? Why?

- Are there some dreams that you have never dared to consider seriously? Why?

What is your life's work?

Answering this question involves reflecting on the kind of work that you find the most rewarding and valuable. It is the work that makes you feel truly alive, joyful and satisfied. It doesn't have to bring you fame or wealth, but it brings out the best in you.

- What are the activities that you love more than your own comfort or convenience?

- What work would you do, even if you weren't paid for it? Why?

- Why are you here?

- What meaning do you find in each day?

- What brings you the most fulfilment?

- What have you done in your life that you are really proud of? Who were you with? What material things did you need? What, if anything, prevents you from repeating this experience or something similar?

- What are your regrets? How can you make sure that you don't give yourself cause for regret in the future?

- What do you need in order to develop your passions, talents and gifts?

What are your priorities from the lists made so far?

Given that you have a limited amount of time left in your life, and a limited amount of energy, you need to prioritise from the lists you have made so far.

- What really matters to you?

- What or who would you put before everything else?

- List your priorities in order of importance. To what extent are you currently able to prioritise the most important?

What do you not want?

This could be the most important question of all. In a multi-choice society, where so much is on offer, it is a mark of discernment and vision to refuse certain paths, which are often presented as essential. Start by making a list of the things you don't want.

- How do you decide when you have enough success, enough professional renown, and enough achievement?

- What are your limits? How do you know when you have reached them?

- How do you distinguish between your wants and your needs?

- What do you need to let go of, in order to have enough for you?

Under what conditions can you create the things your vision has identified as worthwhile?

You probably won't immediately be able to create all the things you have identified as worthwhile, but you can start to think about what would make these things possible. You need to create the conditions in your life that will help you to do the things your vision identified as worthwhile. To do this, you may need to slow down, especially if you are suffering from any kind of stress or overload in your job. Chapter Three, *Slowing the Treadmill of Work*, provides suggestions for getting your working life under control. As Donella Meadows has written, "Time is life, and to go zooming through it is to miss living. Slow down. Do that first. Then, quietly, carefully, think about what else might need to be done." Time gives you the opportunity to discover things about your life, which, although meaningless or invisible to others, can transform it completely.

- What resources do you need?

- What information do you need?

- Who do you need talk to?

- What concrete steps are you capable of taking right now?

- What consequences will changes have? How can you be prepared for these?

These exercises are intended to help you get in touch with what is potentially greatest in you, what Charles Handy refers to as your soul. The answers will be different for everyone, and they may differ for any one person, at different times. The people whose stories feature later may never have done a visioning exercise in exactly this way, but they have all thought about their values, priorities, dreams and what makes them fulfilled. They have also given careful thought to the things they neither want nor need.

The exercises are not intended to create a never-ending "things to do" list, which will never get done and which will make you feel worse every time you look at it. They start with a broad slate concerning your dreams and all the things you could do. But because your lifetime is finite, and because you don't have endless choices, they go on to encourage you to select the most important things from the list, discarding what you don't want or need. You need to set achievable goals in relation to the things you do want, and give yourself a timeframe for putting them into practice.

It is also useful to write or say affirmations concerning your vision, in order to keep it in your mind. For example, you can say to yourself, "I am letting go of the things I don't need", or "I am daily becoming clearer about my priorities", or "I am finding ways to act on my vision", or "I am daily finding ways to acquire the information I need". You may not know how to reach your goals, but concentrating on them by doing regular affirmations makes you sensitive to opportunities to turn them into reality.

Another way to work on something that is really bothering you is to keep a journal. Choose a single issue, and write about it for twenty minutes a day for five days, concentrating on answering the question, "What are my deepest feelings about this issue?" Don't worry about what anybody else would think about it when they read it. You don't show this to anybody. In fact, you don't even need to read it over yourself. Just concentrate on answering the question for twenty minutes, even if you repeat yourself. When you are finished writing, let the subject go from your conscious mind. Try not to think about it until you take up your journal again. This is a powerful process, which I have found very useful at many times in my life. For example, in the middle of writing this book, I found myself at a point of despair. I thought that nobody would want to read it, that it would not be good enough, and that I was making myself vulnerable by writing about these issues. The journal process helped me to deal with these feelings and continue with renewed confidence that the book would be good enough, and that it didn't have to provide all the answers.

Some of the real-life stories may help you devise your own answers to your questions. You could read some of the authors mentioned (all the details are in the *Bibliography*), whom I have found inspirational in working on my own vision. Don't expect answers to come to you all at once. Be open to their arrival when you least expect them, like when you are walking your dog, exercising or doing physical work, playing with your children or interacting with other people, or relaxing in any number of ways. Many people keep an index card or small notebook with them always, so that they can write down the ideas that come to them at times like these. This is a useful habit for anybody working on a life vision.

Take Change Slowly

You may have decided that you want to change your life overnight. This could be fine if you live alone, or have no responsibilities to other people. But consider carefully the consequences of giving up a job, or making some other dramatic change very quickly, even if you are responsible to nobody but yourself. We often believe that we should make major changes quickly, once we have realised what the problem is, but I believe that substantive change is usually the result of carefully planned and manageable moves based on an understanding of the whole problem. Small, incremental changes generally work best with oneself, in relationships, in organisations and in lifestyle. If you start with small changes, you can feel happy that you are doing something about the problem, and you can discuss the changes with the people in your life who will be affected by them. You can also give yourself time to increase your understanding of your life as a whole, and therefore to make the changes most appropriate to your circumstances.

Rework your Vision from Time to Time

You should come back to the vision exercises from time to time, because our visions change, as we work towards them, make mistakes along the way, respond creatively to those mistakes, and learn more about ourselves. Give yourself time for regular reflection. Relax enough to listen to the voices within you that ask for something different. Come back to the question about your own version of *enough*.

You need to regularly set some time aside. Half an hour a day of quiet time away from traffic and crowds, to walk, meditate, or write in a journal, is a good way to develop vision and a sense of purpose. It is not just a rational exercise. You don't simply change your intellectual opinions or learn about new concepts. As you answer the big questions, like "Who am I?" and "Why am I here?", you also exercise your emotions. It is also a spiritual process, because it encourages you to look beyond yourself, to your connections with other people and with the world around you. This process is part of what Charles Handy calls "proper selfishness", whereby we bring out the best in ourselves, so that we can make meaningful contact with others, and be truly human.

Expand Your Vision beyond Yourself and Your Time

Knowledge of human limits is connected to awareness of the planet's limits. We come to understand that we live in an interconnected world, where every aspect of life is connected to the personal search for balance: our patterns of consumption, our living and working arrangements, interpersonal relations, international relations, corporate affairs, education, government, communications media, and many more.

You can also create visions for your family, household, community (neighbourhood community and community of interest), for your country, and for the planet. Humans are, after all, a global species. Dave Ellis also suggests drawing up visions for the long-range future, which extend way beyond your lifetime. Think about visions for fifty, a hundred, even a thousand years hence, which others might consider worthwhile carrying on, even after you are gone. Ask yourself what neighbourhoods could look like, how people would earn a living, how cities might be changed, how life in the countryside might be different, what people might do for entertainment, how children would be cared for, how different groups and nationalities would interact with each other.

Some of these exercises are best done with a group of like-minded people. Everyone can draw up their own vision and share it with the other group members. You don't always have to write ideas, as drawings can be very effective. Set some ground rules first, whereby all visions are listened to without criticism. Don't dismiss other people's visions, even silently, because they may have something to inspire you.

Enjoy the Process

Balanced living is something you arrive at by doing. Until you start doing, you don't understand it, and the more you do it, the more you understand it in your own unique way. Acting on your vision is exciting, because it entails a journey. It is essential to have an end in mind, and your vision provides that, but the journey towards the end is equally important.

It is tempting to believe that you need to achieve all your goals and make your vision real, before you can be happy. But this is not the case. Once you are taking steps, the process of happiness starts. You find reasons to be happy in the present; you enjoy and celebrate the process of getting there, as well as the end point. As the great Brazilian educator Paolo Freire put it, "We make the road by walking". Every step is important. There is no final realm of freedom and balance, so *how* we undertake our journey is just as important as *what* we are aiming for. Bring your vision into every single day and, drawing on it, live as if every day were your last chance to put some part of it into practice.

Chapter Three

SLOWING THE TREADMILL OF WORK

Paid work is *the* central feature of life for many in Ireland today, whether we think of it as just a job, or as a career for life. We tend to take our identities from our paid work, and we describe other people according to the jobs they do. As people try to fit other aspects of life, such as relationships, children and personal development, around their jobs, they often feel stretched to the limit all the time, an experience described by Richard Swenson as overload syndrome.

This chapter makes practical suggestions for putting work into its proper place in your life, so that you can balance it comfortably with the other things that are important to you. It examines basic ideas for getting work under control, so that you can create more time and energy. Downshifting does not always have to take the form of dramatic changes. You don't have to think in terms of giving up a job. Downshifting can take the simple form of shifting down a gear, so that you are not pushing yourself so hard all the time. The suggestions won't all suit you or be appropriate for the kind of work you do, but several will. Some won't make any sense at all just now, but will be meaningful when you come back to this chapter after practising balance for a while.

Work a Forty-Hour Week

Does your workplace have a culture of overwork? Do you cultivate a personal culture of working long hours? Where does it come from? Do your company or you see it as a sign of success to work ten- or twelve-hour days, or longer, and then take work home at weekends? If you work for yourself, it can be as bad or worse. You can set impossibly high expectations that eventually result in overload. Work expands to fill the time allotted for it, so extra time on the job doesn't indicate higher productivity or better quality.

Try leading a quiet change in your workplace culture, so that it becomes the norm to work no more than a forty-hour week. Why not start later in the morning, finish earlier in the evening and take proper breaks? Don't work through lunchtime, but use the time to exercise, meet a friend, meditate or do some other activity not related to the job. Turn down overtime if that's a usual part of your job, and stop taking work home, in order to do extra, or to catch up. Everybody has times when they need to put in some extra effort to meet a deadline, and I'm not suggesting that you should never do this. But it can make a huge difference if you prevent this from becoming your usual way of working, and make forty hours the norm. And even this is too much for some people — cut back as much as you feel is possible.

There's nothing intrinsically wrong with taking work home or working outside regular hours. You may, for instance, choose to take time off in the middle of the day to collect children, meet friends or do some other activity that can't be done in the evening, and then to make up the work time, later in the day or early in the morning. If you work for yourself, you can probably be even more creative in the ways you use the time. For instance, Eoghan Corry and Richard Douthwaite, whose stories are in Chapters Seven and Eight, get most of their deskwork done very early in the mornings, leaving the rest of the day free for physical work or family.

You could also investigate the possibility of working one day from home, or working a five-day week in four days. If you work for yourself, this can often be easily accomplished. And such options are also offered by many companies. The website *www.familyfriendly.ie* is run by the Equality Authority, and gives good suggestions, along with case studies, for both employees and employers. It also explains your statutory rights.

Set Other Boundaries around your Work

Avoid being constantly available for work. Be selective about giving out your mobile phone number or e-mail address. Switch off your mobile phone or pager when you are not at work. If you must take calls outside regular work hours, set limits on when you are available. Ask people not to call you after a certain hour at night or at weekends, unless it is urgent.

Break the habit of responding immediately to e-mails and phone calls. Many people find that they spend much of their day on the phone or dealing with e-mails, and then have to work late or take work home, to get the essential work completed. Set aside a regular time each day for dealing with your post, as well as answering phone calls and e-mails. Remember that they don't all have to be responded to immediately, or even at all. Separate them into "deal with now" and "deal with later" categories. Aim to keep the "deal with later" pile as small as possible, and allow time to return to it when you have the information to do so, or when the time is appropriate.

Control interruptions and go to work areas that are quiet, if you need uninterrupted time. Be discerning about new technologies that make you more accessible. Why not investigate some that actually block interruptions? Get your name taken off junk mail lists. Unsubscribe from e-mail discussion groups that you don't have time to keep up with. Ask to be taken off unnecessary automatic e-mail lists. Elaine St James' book, *Simplify Your Work Life*, is worth reading for its many excellent suggestions.

Most of us keep a diary of some sort, but many tend to enter only job-related appointments. Time for oneself, for friends and for family should also be entered in the same diary, and should be regarded as equal in importance to job-related appointments.

Learn to Switch Off

Some of us find it hard to switch off, and to stop thinking about work, even when we are physically removed from it, but this is an essential part of the setting of boundaries. Many people achieve it through exercise or play outside of work time, but it is also useful to be able to do it for short periods in the workplace. Learn to take mental "time out" for a few seconds, by relaxing your body and breathing deeply. Regular meditation or practices such as yoga or t'ai chi are very good daily ways to give your mind a break.

At the end of each day, it is a good idea to take five minutes to arrange your desk or work area. Put away materials you have finished using, or straighten up things you will use when you start again. Think of what needs to be done for the next day, and where you will start. You could leave a note to yourself, prioritising the next day's tasks. Elaine St James points out that this process is a review of the day just finished, which makes you aware of what you have achieved. It is also a signal to your mind that the day's work is finished, and that you can leave it and get on with the rest of your activities. A ritual like this is also a method of handing over the work to your subconscious mind, which will deal with it creatively, even while you are doing other things, so that you can work productively and effectively when you start again.

Sometimes when you are involved in a project, creative ideas for it will come into your mind when you are relaxing, doing other work, dropping off to sleep at night, or when you wake in the morning. It's useful to keep a notebook by your bed, or index cards around the house or in your pocket, so that you can record these ideas and then get back to whatever you are doing, safe in the knowledge that you won't forget them.

Set Reasonable Deadlines

Set reasonable deadlines for your projects. When asked how long something will take, give yourself time for unexpected delays and to work at a reasonable pace. Avoid taking on too many projects at once, explaining to your employer, boss or client that it is impossible to deal with all of them to a high standard. Don't be afraid to ask for time to think about your capacity to take on another project. If you work for a company whose culture makes changes like these very difficult, start looking for another employer that understands the importance of personal and family time. Take time to talk to other employees in companies where you go for interview. Find out what the culture is really like, and if it differs from management's descriptions of it.

If you are self-employed, it is equally important not to take on too many projects at once. It can actually command respect if you explain that you are not able to take on a new project, because you cannot devote the necessary time to it. It implies that you take your projects seriously. It may also help if you suggest a time in the future when you will be free to take on new work.

Cut down on Commuting Time

If you already work from home, you probably rejoice at the time saved commuting. If you are commuting two or three hours or more a day, you need to consider the alternatives. Is it possible to move closer to your job, without increasing your housing expenses? If yes, it's worth discussing it with the people you live with, who would also be affected by the move. If a move is not on, could you find a job closer to home, in order to cut down on commuting time? Consider the options, and even if a change is not possible at the moment, keep it in your consciousness. You never know what possibilities may arise closer to home. One woman I met while researching this book had a two-hour commute, but was offered a job five minutes' drive from her home, although for a salary of £10,000 (€12,700) a year less. She took it, reasoning that she would have an extra four hours for herself and her children each day, and she is very pleased with the change.

If you cannot actually shorten your commuting journey, maybe you could shorten the time it takes, by starting and finishing work at off-peak times, when traffic is lighter. If you normally commute by car, and there are public transport options, you could investigate them. They may be quicker, and they often allow you to read, work or doze, which you cannot do while driving. If you use the time to work, be careful that this does not become a regular, unpaid, extension of working hours. Cycling is an option you could also consider. Many people are reluctant to consider public transport or cycling options, because they concentrate on the dis-advantages. But you need to be open to considering the advantages too.

Be Discriminating about Information

Be discriminating about the amount and quality of information you require. Many of us are "drowning in data", in the words of Richard Swenson. We think we need far more information than we actually do, in order to do our jobs well. The explosion in data is straining all the systems trying to deal with it. Many of us subscribe to paper and electronic journals and other publications that we can never read completely. We don't remember most of the information we do come across, unless we are using it in a meaningful context. But many of us see information in our field moving so fast that we panic because we can't keep up with it. We also put pressure on ourselves and other people to take educational courses, in order to keep up, or to stay ahead. We need to learn when to stop.

Be selective about information. Most of it dates fairly quickly, because it is not of high quality. Many books and articles are written simply to get someone's name in print, or to satisfy demands that they publish. Understand what you need to get your job done well and be ruthless about discarding the rest.

Don't take on extra courses unless you are truly interested in the subject matter. Even then, look for courses that use methodologies that help you to explore information and search for meaningful ways to use it, rather than relying on memory.

Understand that it is okay not to know, in many circumstances. By giving yourself permission not to know, you can let go of fears that you will be exposed as ignorant or incompetent.

Cancel subscriptions to journals and other publications, including newspapers, which you don't have time to read. Stop stockpiling them, thinking that you will get round to reading them at weekends or holidays. If you don't have time to read them today, it is highly unlikely that you will read them in the future. Get rid of piles that have accumulated. "The consequences on your career of missing several months of journal articles will not be measurable, while the positive effects on your mental health may be considerable," observes Richard Swenson. "Anything important that was in the pile of journals you tossed will reappear in the next pile."

When you do receive quality information, file or store it in a place where you can easily retrieve it. Work on the principle of handling things only once. If you find that you have little piles of information all over the place, consider how long they have been there. Are you going to miss them if you get rid of them? Probably not. If you think you will, put them all in a box, and date the box. If you still haven't missed them after two months, shred them.

The Internet is a marvellous tool for research and communication. But for many people, time spent online is time wasted. Much of the information it provides is low quality. Work out how to use it to your best advantage. Avoid letting any of your Internet behaviours become addictive, by avoiding excessive e-mail use, web surfing, online games and chat rooms.

Understand the difference between information and useful knowledge. Certain kinds of information are indeed essential, but having information does not guarantee that someone will use it wisely. Knowledge is something we create for ourselves. It includes a wise use of information, so that we can do our jobs well. It changes and grows, depending on our circumstances. You need limited amounts of information, but unlimited knowledge, in order to do your work well.

Take Holidays

Do you find that you don't always use up your holiday allowance? Some workers are actually proud that they don't take all of their allowance, or that they contact their workplace every day while they are on holiday. Ask yourself how that approach is of benefit to you and your holiday companions. As a start, don't brag about not taking your holidays. Take every single day that's due to you, including time in lieu, if this is part of your contract, and arrange things so that you do not phone or contact your workplace while you are on holiday.

You don't have to go away from home in order to justify taking holiday time. Time spent at leisure at home is equally good for you. In fact, holidaying from a home base, going for day trips, eating out or cooking leisurely meals at home, seeing friends, visiting local attractions, having time to read good books, or going to the theatre and cinema, can provide a very pleasant break, without the stress and expense of going away.

You could also extend your annual holiday allowance by taking one or two weeks' unpaid leave. You will need to negotiate this with an employer, making it clear that you don't expect to be paid for the time off, and explaining how and when you will take the time, so that it is not disruptive to your organisation. Many jobs in the public service now allow workers with children under eighteen to take extended unpaid leave in the summer. The Parental Leave Act also now allows parents to take unpaid leave while children are young.

If you work for yourself, it's equally important to take holidays. Don't make the mistake of thinking you can't afford to. You can't afford not to, with regard to your health and relationships.

Don't Go to Work when You Are Ill

What is to be gained by going to work when you have a bad cold or 'flu? You will get very little work done and, by the end of the day, you may well feel worse and will probably have passed on your bug to several other people. It is far better for your own health and a speedy recovery, and more responsible to other people, to take adequate time off, until you are properly recovered.

Don't Travel for Work unless Absolutely Necessary

Travelling to meetings can sometimes take up far more time than the value of the meeting warrants. Try to do as much work as possible via video conferencing, telephone and e-mail links. If you decide that the journey really is worthwhile, use the train if at all possible, because you can probably do some work *en route*, and avoid it piling up back at your workplace.

Conferences can also sound attractive and are sometimes worthwhile. But again, be discriminating about how many you attend. Try to avoid travelling to conferences during personal and family time. For example, try to travel on Monday rather than on Sunday, so that the weekend remains your own. And avoid spending Sunday preparing for travel and the conference ahead. Workers often come under pressure to be away at weekends for this kind of work, because air travel is cheaper if there is a Saturday night stopover. Also, many such conferences are on at weekends. It can sometimes be nice to have weekend time at a foreign venue, but if you find it becoming a strain, resist whenever you can.

Question the Real Monetary Value of Longer Hours

Some jobs don't pay any extra for working long hours. It may be part of your contract that you work the number of hours necessary to do the job. But if working a shorter week means turning down overtime or turning down freelance projects or clients, you may feel that you can't afford it. But many people find that the longer hours they work, the more they spend on convenience foods and services, or on "rewards" to themselves, such as clothes, therapies like massage, or short hotel breaks. You also pay tax on the extra income, so don't forget to calculate that. Losing out on the income may not affect you, if you don't need those extras that make it possible for you to put in the long hours. If you calculate that you really could benefit financially from extra work, you may decide that it's worth it for a while, in order to pay off debts, or to accumulate savings. But you should also set a time to review this way of working. Avoid letting it become a habit.

"I Love My Work"

Many of us are highly driven, and if you are one of those people, you may be thinking right now that these ideas are very sensible, but for other people, not for you. Maybe your paid work is in a caring profession and you feel it's more like a vocation. Or perhaps it is very stimulating and you really enjoy it. It can be difficult to look on such work as a mere job. There are people who are energised by their work and are prepared to put in sixty- and seventy-hour weeks. You may ask if there is anything wrong with working very long hours if you love the work. However, it is impossible to work these kinds of hours and have sufficient time and energy for a balanced life that includes friends, family, nutritious food, exercise and some time doing nothing.

Even if you don't work more than forty hours per week at the job you love, are you spending all your time on the job doing the work you want? Or are you doing administration, or fund-raising, or some other activity essential to the survival of your organisation, but which also keeps you away from the work that attracted you to the job in the first place? Do you have to do types of work you don't particularly like, because you are getting paid for the job, or, if you run your own business and employ other people, are you working to support your staff?

Many of the people who tell their stories in this book also love their work, in the broadest sense of the term "work". But they have broken the bond that always links it to pay. Suppose you had no or minimal debts, and minimal living expenses, and didn't need the money it brings you? Would you still do your job? If the answer is yes, that's great, and you are lucky to have work you love. But if you didn't need the pay, would you do it in a different way? Would you approach the actual work differently?

"My Work is Very Important"

Another excuse for spending too long on the job is that your work is helping to save the world and the people in it. Paid or unpaid, many highly committed activists take the moral high ground and become workaholics with too many commitments. Donella Meadows, the American activist, writer and teacher, recognised this tendency in herself, and suggested that the world would be a better place if everybody slowed down, including those trying to save it. She quotes Thomas Merton, the Trappist priest, who said, "The frenzy of the activist neutralises his work for peace. It destroys the fruitfulness of his own work, because it kills the root of inner wisdom which makes work fruitful." Could this apply to you? Ann Louise Gilligan, whose story is below, describes how she combines a full-time academic job with community activism.

೩ ೩ ೩

Ann Louise Gilligan
Activism, academia and spirit

Since the 1970s, Ann Louise Gilligan has combined community activism with academic life. In 1976, she took up a post as lecturer, first in Religious Studies and more recently in Education, at St Patrick's College, Drumcondra, Dublin. In 1986, she and Katherine Zappone set up The Shanty Educational Project, to provide educational opportunities for women on low incomes in the Tallaght area of west Dublin. The project is now community-owned and is run by a Board of 21 people, some of whom are local residents and others who are committed women and men from outside the area.

The Shanty was based for many years at Katherine and Ann Louise's home in Brittas, and Ann Louise was its executive director until 2001. They put a lot of their own money and professional time into the project when it started. Recently, the project secured government funding to build a Centre for education, enterprise and childcare for the people of West Tallaght, located in a new million-pound building called An Cosán.

Combining her different roles has required a balancing act over the years. "I feel if one is going to sustain a commitment as an activist and an academic, you can't live out of those two worlds, and achieve what people could in either of them alone," she explains. In her lecturing post, she has chosen to prioritise teaching over publishing, in contrast to the emphasis of many academics. "I think good, prepared teaching is so important," she explains. She says that she has never bought into the academic pressure to "publish or perish". "I don't experience it; I'm not driven in that sense. I'd love to have a bit more published, but if I don't, I can let it go."

Nevertheless, there was a time when the balancing act failed to hold together. In 1993, Ann Louise found herself in a situation that was "really quite fraught", with a lot of work in the Shanty and tensions in her academic post. Around the same time, she found that she had breast cancer. "I had to re-visit a lot of things. First of all, I revisited the work situation and I was determined I wasn't leaving my profession, because I didn't want to leave the students and that whole context; however, I was clear that I needed to change departments." As this was being negotiated, she was on leave for two years, during which time she concentrated on her healing and writing. "Getting cancer, I was really alerted to reflecting on my life, and I made radical changes. I call it a turning point. I wanted to live and, thank God, it was in its very earliest stages. I was very lucky. At that time, I took up a fairly serious pattern of meditation and I found that extremely important in my healing and I continue it," she says.

"I also had to look at the fact that our home, which was the centre of the Shanty project, had really become a community centre," she continues. "Although at this stage it had moved out of our own living room to the mews behind our house, still, you could never come downstairs in your nightdress! I had to revisit that, and I certainly wasn't going to pull the plug on the project. In fact some of us were battling very hard with the County Council to get land to build on for An Cosán, so it wasn't the time to pull back. But I was really faced with a dilemma, so I bought myself a beautiful log cabin, which is way over in this field beside our house. That was a huge solace. I'm actually not attached to possessions, except my log cabin. It's my office at home, and it has a wood burning stove, and I meditate, write and reflect there. That was one of the first things I did when I became ill. I suddenly had a distance between home and this all-enveloping project.

"A deep commitment to a spiritual dimension of life and, in an equal way, a commitment to a relational life" have guided Ann Louise's work and helped her create a balance between her paid and unpaid work, her academic and activist lives, over the years. She has striven for praxis, which she describes as "reflection-action in the spiritual sense, but then reversing that, so that into one's activism one brings the practice of the spiritual. The imagination has also been at the heart of my interest and I have a huge personal commitment to the development of imagination and to really trying to foster and live out of that faculty. I think if we could educate people to believe in their imaginative, creative capacity, we would have a different world.

"In setting up the Shanty, Katherine and I always held that the heart of this project is something about love and spirituality that I believe continues to sustain it. Many of the women, when they talk about coming to courses — it wouldn't always be so much the content of the course, but what they would remember was the love they felt and the beauty. I feel committed to creating a space that is beautiful. And that, I think, connects us to the holy. We begin every course with an opening circle, a quiet time."

She says that the practice of the spiritual is probably a bit unusual within a community development project. "But many of our original management team who joined us 15 years ago are still with the project in a variety of ways, and it would be their opinion that the relational and the spiritual dimension present among us as a group of people who had a huge variety of backgrounds was something that held us together. Every second Wednesday, we as a management team would meet for what we called a spirituality night. In the beginning, Katherine or I would give an input on some theory or whatever, but then it moved into everybody sharing the responsibility. We'd take a reading and we'd read together, reflect together."

Ann Louise cut back on her commitments during 2001, in a continuation of her search for balance. She has recently let go of her leadership role in An Cosán, and, having finished a research consultancy, is pleased to be able to concentrate on teaching again. Recently she established and now directs a new Educational Disadvantage Centre in St Patrick's College, work that is dear to her heart. She takes regular exercise and all of her holiday allowance. She does not see herself retiring in the conventional sense, although she might not go on in her salaried post to the official retirement age. "I certainly don't believe in that kind of ageist countdown. I think that we might develop another project — we talk about that, both of us. But what I do visualise is a change, where I could have more time just to think and write. I think 'being lazy' is probably a very positive concept in this day and age. It allows a self-focus and a self-indulgence in the positive sense that isn't otherwise permitted. I hope I'm going to get back more and more to that as I grow older.

"I think there are very few people who have been fortunate enough to have had what I have, by way of starting here in 1976 and not struggling with unemployment. It is a very privileged place to be. We have a house and a little place in Kerry. So what we have sustains. I mean, what's a simple lifestyle? I see people and work with people who live with great dignity in terrible poverty. I see education as a key to the transformation of poverty, and our work in Tallaght seeks to concretise that vision. Furthermore, it keeps before us the constant challenge to share our resources and our privilege. I certainly don't think we live in any wasteful way. I have what I need, which is an extraordinary gift. But I hope I have shared what I have. That would be very important to me.

"I'm not trying to paint a picture that every day is kind of calm and balanced," she says. "I think a commitment to try to live out one's unique calling really is a journey. It is a spiritual kind of thing. I certainly have not arrived; however, I have a commitment to a life that nourishes stillness and quiet."

Ann Louise's tip: "I would say, if you are ever going to set up something, do it in partnership with somebody. Don't dream of trying to do something on your own. I have seen too many people try that and it's not worked out very well. Try to have some kind of sharing of the leadership."

ೋ ೋ ೋ

Chapter Four

SLOWING THE TREADMILL EVEN MORE

The suggestions in Chapter Three for getting work under control are relatively low-risk. They focus on managing your job in ways that won't have much effect on your income. This chapter contains suggestions for going a bit further, looking at working part-time, freelancing or even giving up paid work altogether.

Getting paid work under control, in both low-risk and radical ways, is often presented as a "family-friendly" move, suitable for women who want to combine paid work and caring for children. But it is a mistake to assume that men with children and individuals who have no children would not benefit from taking up some of these options also. It is true that many parents today are walking a tightrope between job and family, but it is not just family commitments combined with paid work that leave us feeling burnt out. These options are also people-friendly, and if parents are the only ones to take them up, they will not be seen as relevant to all of us.

Slowing down is beneficial to everybody, because it creates more time to listen to and care for all the other people with whom we have contact, including work colleagues, friends, children and other family members. We don't make so many mistakes, and if we do make mistakes, they are not so crucial, and there's time to rectify them, as well as time to learn from them.

If you think you cannot afford such changes, for a start, you could think about sharing the financial burden with another adult in your household. Then consider that you may even save money, because you won't need "time-saving" commodities and services.

Work Three or Four Days, Job Share or Work Part-Time

These options involve working a shorter number of hours per week than is the norm in your organisation. With job sharing, you will need to find somebody to do the other half of your job. Many organisations now have policies on job-sharing and, although it's usually seen as an option for women with children, there is absolutely no reason why men shouldn't take it also.

Job-sharing works better in some occupations than in others. For instance, primary-school teachers are often able to work one week on, one week off. However, second-level teachers often find that, in order to suit the timetable, they need to be in school four days, or that they have classes at the beginning and end of a day, but the time in-between is not enough to travel home. Check it out carefully before making a decision.

Working four days or part-time may be more difficult to organise, as your organisation may not have policies on it. When discussing it with the relevant people, be clear about why you want to work like this, and how it could be organised so that both you and the organisation benefit. You can also visit the Equality Authority website, *www.familyfriendly.ie*, to find out about your statutory rights, and how they affect both employers and employees. If you work part-time, you may still have full commuting time, so you need to decide it this is worthwhile.

You could also investigate the possibility of working ten months and spreading your salary over twelve months, so that you have an income each month. This will allow you to take an extra-long holiday, which can be useful if you want to travel or do some other block activity.

One of the disadvantages that people mention about working like this is that you may find yourself left out of crucial networks, both formal and informal. You may find yourself staying on, or coming in during time off, in order to attend a crucial meeting. You will need to decide when and if this is worth it, or you could decide to accept the disadvantages of being out of the networks. Be careful also to establish just what work you are now responsible for. Make sure that you are not expected to do the same work in less time.

Avoid Promotion or Make a Downward Move

Promotion to a more demanding position may make the difference between having a job that is perfectly manageable and having one that is stressful and pressurised. Avoiding promotion or giving it up, if a new position is not working out, are excellent balancing strategies.

A disadvantage associated with not going for promotion is that you may be viewed as not committed to the company or as lacking in ambition. If you want to make a downward move, you may be seen as weak or no longer able for the pressure. Nevertheless, these decisions can be immensely liberating. While researching this book, I met several people who had decided not to apply for promotion and several others who regretted taking on more responsible posts. I also met three people who had taken downward moves. They don't wish their stories to appear in the book, but they are all very pleased with their moves.

If you have your heart set on a promotion, ask yourself about the extra pressures it will entail. Will there be more administrative work, and less of the hands-on work that you are good at and that you like? Will you be "in over your head"? Will you need to work longer hours in order to cope? Many people find that promotion plays havoc with their relationships, because of the extra time they have to devote to the new work. Will the status and the money outweigh all of these new pressures?

If you want to make a downward move, that is, to give up the management part of your job, be prepared for people to regard you suspiciously. Again, think carefully about your reasons before making a move. Make a list of advantages and disadvantages, both to yourself and to the company, but when making your case, present only the advantages. Timing and talking to the right people can be crucial in making a move like this work smoothly.

Become a Portfolio Worker

Portfolio working is the term used to describe people whose work includes a mixture of part-time jobs, temporary, contract, freelance, consulting or self-employment. It allows you to have several sources of income, from a collection of different clients, customers and employers, so that you are not dependent on any one source for income. Many portfolio workers feel more secure than those who depend on one employer for all of their income. Working like this allows you to use your talents in a variety of settings and to work to schedules that suit you. As well as that, it facilitates you to do some of the work as "gift work" for organisations who cannot afford a fee, but whose ideals you support.

Portfolio working is not a new concept for all those people who have always relied on freelance work. Actors, journalists, electricians, plumbers, writers, musicians and gardeners are just a few whose money comes from lots of different sources. They have all had to learn to manage their time and money independently of employment. If you are considering such a step, you will need to do some research on work and work settings that will suit you. If you are in a job, you might like to stay in it on a part-time basis, at least initially, while taking on a variety of other work. In that case, you will need to make the case to your employer, as outlined in the previous section.

Be very careful not to take on too many freelance contracts at once. One of the biggest challenges involved is turning down work. You don't sell your time in advance, the way you do with a conventional job, so offers of work are very much in the present. It can be difficult to turn them down because of the fear that you won't get work when you need it. But it can be disastrous if you take on too many projects and cannot deliver on them. As discussed in Chapter Three ("Set Reasonable Deadlines"), it can command respect from a potential client if you explain that you cannot take on a project, because you can't devote sufficient time to it at present. It may also be helpful if you are able to suggest a time in the future when you will be free to take it on or, if you can, refer your potential client to another portfolio worker. Some of the other ideas in Chapter Three are also relevant for keeping portfolio work within boundaries.

Devise good ways to decide how much time a particular project will need. When asked how long a project will take, it is not a good idea to give an immediate answer. Elaine St James recommends that you take time to list everything involved in the job. Be sure to consult other people from whom you will need information and resources, because it is often the case that they cannot give them to you exactly when you would like them. Estimate how long all of that will take. Then take into account all the other projects you will be involved with at the same time. Make a new estimate — and then double it. Only then, advises St James, are you ready to commit to a completion date.

Portfolio working can sometimes be lonely, so it is a good idea to join networks. Through them, you may find work and you can pass on projects for which you do not have the time, the inclination or the skills. You can share information and learn new skills, and you may occasionally work in partnership with somebody else from the network.

If you decide that this kind of work arrangement is for you, and you haven't had income from self-employment before, you will need to learn about the tax system and how it applies to workers who have a mixture of self-employed and pay-as-you-earn income. Colm Rapple's annual financial guide, *Family Finance*, is a good place to start. Brian O'Kane's book, *Starting a Business in Ireland*, and its accompanying website, also provide excellent advice. You will need to be organised about keeping records of expenses and income. Before starting out, it would also be a good idea to have a minimum of debt, or no debts at all. If you have a mortgage, it is a good idea to have one source of income that is pretty certain and regular. Apart from mortgages, most freelance workers and portfolio workers avoid taking on the type of personal debt that requires monthly repayments. Instead, they save and purchase when they can afford it.

The benefits of portfolio working are strong. Apart from not relying on a single source of income, you also have the advantage of being able to work flexibly, at times and places to suit you, and to take on projects you enjoy. Charles Handy also recommends the "creative chunking" that portfolio working allows, where you work more-or-less full-time for a period of, say, six or nine months, and then have three or more months free to pursue some unpaid work or interest that needs blocks of time. Handy also points out that you will be able to do paid work for longer as a portfolio worker than if you are in conventional employment, and therefore don't need to worry about building up a huge pension fund. His books, *The Hungry Spirit* and *The Elephant and the Flea*, are interesting reading for anyone thinking of pursuing these options.

Maximise your Income from Paid Work

It makes sense to get the maximum return from any paid work you do. Work is much more than your job and it does not always have to mean paid work. The purpose of doing work for pay is to create sufficient income to meet your material needs and the needs of those dependent on you. Maximising your income is different from a "more is better" philosophy, which wants to accumulate ever-more money and material goods. In order to live a balanced life, you need a certain amount of money, to buy the possessions you need. But after you have enough, you do not need money as a source of status, satisfaction or identity. Once your material needs are met, then you can concentrate on your life work.

Paid work is also essential if you need to get out of debt, or want to finance activities like study, personal development, or travel. You might also want to develop savings and investments so that you can become financially independent and give up paid work altogether in the future. To get the best return on the energy you put into your paid work, you need to earn the maximum amount compatible with your integrity and your health, as suggested by Joe Dominguez and Vicki Robin. If your income at the end of a week or a month does not reflect the effort and life-energy you put into the work (and only you can judge this), then you need to consider what to do.

If you are employed, you might need to get a new, higher-paid job. For self-employed workers, it could mean increasing your rates. Don't price your work too low. If you do, you will need to take on too many jobs, you will be too pressed to do quality work, and the market for your work will fall off. "It is a mistake to assume that a competitive price is the only determinant of market success," writes Charles Handy. "It can be one way of pricing oneself too low and out of contention in the future. Quality can matter more than price, but quality costs money to start with." Eoghan Corry, whose story features in Chapter Seven, offers this advice: "Don't undercharge. Always charge well, and if you really have to, if you really like someone, and they can't afford you, work for nothing. They'll get embarrassed coming back and asking you to work for nothing. Or else, their business will thrive, and they will be able to offer you work and pay you properly for it. But if you start working for very little, they'll expect you to do it all the time."

Maximising your income also means reducing job-related expenses, such as clothing, transport and food, which detract from your net income. Ask yourself if you could do different work, or work differently, in ways that would not incur those expenses (see "How Much Does Your Job Cost You?" in Chapter Six).

Explore Entrepreneurial Opportunities

If it suits your personality, you could start your own business, doing something you like and can do well. But be careful. Be wary of ads for home-based businesses that you run for other people or businesses that require you to know a lot of people. Begin by taking a look at yourself, and be realistic. Compare your skills and resources to the demands of the business. If you want to work from home, do you have enough space? Do you have the necessary equipment? Do you have enough cash to start up, and to last until you begin to get paid?

Be careful to avoid enterprises that need a lot of money to get started. The goal is to make money, not spend it. Also avoid businesses that depend on sales to friends and family. Would the business be compatible with the way of life you want? Consult supportive family and friends, who may have insights about you and your abilities that you have overlooked. Find out about any necessary licences or insurance. Make a realistic projection of what would be enough monthly profit from the business.

Beware also of the notion that if the business is your own, the work will not dominate your life. It may give you more control over your work, but the temptations will still be there to work long hours, skip holidays and be constantly on call. And you may buy into the myth that it's okay, simply because you are doing this for your own business. You will also almost inevitably reach a point where you will have to decide whether to "grow" your business or not. Conventional wisdom says that you should expand, but ask yourself if you really want all that that entails.

Rose O'Sullivan:
Limiting the Growth of a Business

Rose O'Sullivan is in her early thirties and has been running an organic-vegetable box round for three years in West Dublin/Kildare, delivering local produce each week to 200 households. It is currently making her a comfortable living and she has decided not to let it grow it beyond this point.

Rose thinks that if she lets the round grow, it could become too much for one person. Several friends and advisers told her that she should grow it to its fullest potential and employ other people. She considered this option for a while, but decided against it. "I decided that if I take on somebody else, I would need to buy another van, or have the use of another van, and I'd need to double the round. If you do all that, and then if the other person rings in sick, what do you do? I couldn't justify that kind of hassle in my life, not when I can make a decent living doing it on my own." She decided to hold her customers at 200. Her decision was also influenced by the fact that increasing the numbers would mean the farm could not supply all the produce and she would have to find other sources.

Keeping her customer numbers steady also means she can do all her deliveries in four days. "I started doing that because I used to get really hassled — you know, doing the deliveries five days a week and trying to get to the bank and trying to do little things like my grocery shopping and credit union. So I thought I'd just take a day off, to do all that sort of thing. It was really easy. I do 70 people on Tuesday. I used to be out until all hours when I first started doing it, but not now. So on Mondays, I get up a little bit later and I don't consider it a workday. I really consider it a day off. It's lovely. By the time I'm finished on Wednesday, half my week is over. I'm nearly there, after two days' work. When you start work on a Tuesday and you're finished on a Friday, it's great."

Keeping the number at 200 also means that Rose doesn't have to worry about losing people occasionally, which might be the case if she had to maintain 400. She turns away potential customers, in order to keep her numbers steady, and doesn't operate a waiting list. "When I have a space to fill, I just give it to someone I've met that day." She explains that it's simpler and less work to operate that way. She has also stopped delivering to customers she doesn't like. "I just don't anymore," she says. "It's not like I want everyone to be really lovely, but I want to feel comfortable with them. When I feel like just another delivery person, I just couldn't be bothered."

Satisfied with her own round, and not anxious to grow it, she has helped others to start organic-box rounds. "Basically, they rang me up. One of them was a total stranger; he introduced himself, and he said, I know this sounds awful, but I want to start a box round in south Dublin and I heard you're doing one. And I said, grand, I'll meet you in the pub and I'll tell you what you need to know. He came out with me a couple of days, did some work experience, and he started up himself. I gave him all the tips, all the ins and outs. And he was saying, there's not very many people that would share their secrets, you know."

ॐ ॐ ॐ

Take Early Retirement or Voluntary Redundancy

Opportunities for early retirement often arise as organisations downsize. They are also available in certain professions, and in some public service organisations. The amount of pension will vary, depending on the individual circumstances, but even if it's not a full pension, don't assume that you could not live on it. If you get your finances in order, using the suggestions in Chapters Six and Nine, and are accustomed to living within your means, you could be poised to take advantage of an opportunity like this.

Voluntary redundancy is not as financially attractive as early retirement, because there is no pension. But there will be a lump sum, which could help consolidate your finances. And in the case of both retirement and redundancy, you will always have the option of doing freelance work. If you are accustomed to living well within your means, and know how much money you need, you may well reap the benefits of a situation like this.

Doc:
Benefiting from Early Life-Choices

Doc retired in 1996 at the age of 37, from a job that gave him a great deal of satisfaction, as an engineer with a semi-state body. He could afford to take early retirement, because of choices he made early in his life. He has always lived very comfortably, but has been careful with his money. "My pension income is a quarter of what my salary would be if I was working, which is enough for me," he says. "While I was working, my lifestyle never expanded to fill my ample earnings. I have never owned a car, for example. But it's not because I couldn't afford one. I know how to drive, and I hire one when I need it." The source of his income has changed, but not his lifestyle, he says. "I'm still saving money. But I'm not reluctant to spend money either. I just spent a thousand pounds on a brand new bicycle — and people are going, *a thousand pounds on a bicycle,* but that bicycle is something I really wanted, and it's lovely. If it's something I want, I'll buy it. But I'll mull over it, and ask myself if it's really worth it." He is currently undertaking a PhD in climate control. "I wanted change, and I didn't have to decide if the project was financially rewarding or not. It was engineering, but nothing that I had done before, so it's a whole new learning for me."

Doc actively maximised his opportunities from a young age. "We lived over a shop in Dublin 7. I won't say I have a poor background, but I didn't have a rich one — three boys to a room, that kind of stuff. The neighbourhood was middle class-ish. I mean, I'm really lucky that I made all those choices — the right spirit guides and the right choices for me. I never got into the rent trap, which is a huge thing. You have to earn so much, just to have a place to live." He studied for an engineering diploma rather than a degree, because he could begin to earn earlier, and he finished his degree part-time, while working at his first job. As soon as he had some savings, Doc bought a house in a partnership arrangement with his elder brother, in the early 1980s.

Within a year of starting his first job, he was "sold", with the campus company he worked for, to a semi-state body. He stayed there for a while, then worked in the private sector for a time, and then saw an advertisement for "very interesting job as a vision engineer" in his old semi-state organisation. "So nine months later I came back there and effectively went from technician to middle-senior professional in nine months. Three years later, I was at the glass ceiling, the only thing above that was management and I didn't want that." After some restructuring of semi-state bodies in the late 80s, Doc was transferred into a telecom job. "That was fine for a while, lots of international travel and so on, but it was not what I really wanted to be doing. I like real engineering, and it was too much paperwork. Shortly afterwards, they introduced their first retirement package and I applied. But I was too valuable to the new department, so they wouldn't let me go."

Having been refused the retirement, Doc decided he'd like to be job-sharing by forty. "I thought, I don't need all this

money. Earning it takes up all this time. I was in my late twen-
ties then and job-sharing seemed like a nice target for ten
years' time. I decided to get a house of my own and have it
paid for in that time." He didn't have to seek job-sharing,
however, as a second round of retirements came on stream
and he was accepted in 1996. When it was granted, he actually
found it difficult to make up his mind. He had a year to think
about it. "I questioned — why should I take retirement? I have
a really great job, I set my job targets, get paid loads of money,
travel all around Europe, six weeks holidays and, within limits, come and go when I please. If I get sick, I get paid. I had
one of the best jobs you could have. In retrospect, though, the
right question is: why would you *not* do it?"

Before retiring, he left the partnership with his brother
and bought his own house, close to his childhood home.
Later, he used his retirement gratuity to pay off the mortgage.
He is very aware that many working-class people don't have
the chances he has had, because they often lack education and
opportunities to earn good money, and/or they are caught in
a rent trap. He was able to provide a chance for friends who
were in a rent trap, when he went to Holland for ten months.
"I said to them, you can have my house for ten months rent-
free. All you've to do is collect the mail. So that was the deal. I
was interested to see would they save money. And they did,
but that was probably their only chance, and they took it."

"I have plans," he says, "but I could happily scrap every
one of them." He will finish his PhD, but does not want to go
into teaching. "I'll see what comes up. I may well continue
doing some research, if it's interesting." He now has a one-
year-old daughter and people have suggested he will need to
buy a car to transport her, but he disagrees. "I don't want a
car, I'm happy to take her on the bike and she gets a kick from
that," he says. "It's not the first time I carried a kid to school
on my bicycle, on the way to work. You don't need a car for
that."

"I don't view myself as having changed," he concludes.
"Right from the start, I was thinking differently. I've always

had a good idea of what I wanted, whereas it appears to me that most people have done the classic thing — expand their lifestyles to match their income. So first, they have to earn more money, to buy ever-increasing amounts of stuff. And second, they don't know anything else to do. They're in a comfort zone and there's a huge inertia."

‽ ‽ ‽

"Change Back"

When you make changes in the way you do your paid work, especially within an organisation, be prepared for other people to be upset. Even with the low-risk options, which mainly involve setting boundaries around your job to prevent it from taking over your life, you will encounter resentment, either spoken or unspoken. Your colleagues will resent the fact that you are upsetting the status quo, even if they don't quite express it like that. Although they know you are being paid for part-time or other shorter-hours work, they will still be upset by your absences. Watch out for all sorts of "change back" messages. Be clear and confident about your changed ways of working. If you get the opportunity to explain them, say that they are for your own benefit. Don't indulge in overt critique of the organisation or even suggest that others should do as you are doing. If you need to talk about the organisation, preferably do it in confidence with someone you trust who is outside of it, or at least is able to see it objectively.

Your family or other intimates may also give you subtle "change back" messages. Even if they have complained in the past about your absences, they will have developed their own ways of coping. It may not be immediately clear to them that it is an advantage to have you around more often.

When you make changes like these, you are challenging systems that have their own dynamics. They operate like a dance, which you are part of and where everybody knows the familiar steps or patterns. The dynamics may not always be particularly healthy, but they work, after a fashion. If you change the steps in the dance, be prepared for the dynamics to change too and all sorts of unexpected issues to arise. Take things gently. Communicate with other people about why you want change, but without assigning blame.

You may even sabotage your own steps towards change. We find happiness in our choices in the wider world, but the best rational plans can be undermined by spontaneous actions or decisions whose sources are in our unconscious psyches. Planned rational change goes hand in hand with psychic change and we often fail to acknowledge the importance of emotional responses.

You need to take care of your emotional life, as you change your work life and other external parts of your life. Learn to recognise where you are getting emotional satisfaction or some kind of payoff from a fraught lifestyle, and how these will change when you change external things. Many people derive a buzz from having a full diary, or from being unavailable, or from being constantly in demand. Short-term counselling, coaching or supervision can provide useful support. These options usually cost money, however. A low-cost option is to form a group of like-minded people who are capable of supporting each other, without pressure or blame. My book, *Feminist Ways of Knowing*, explores these issues as they pertain to gender equality. I have also found that *The Dance of Anger*, by Magda Goldhor Lerner to be very good on systems and change. Its primary focus is courageous acts of change for women in intimate relationships, but it also contains wonderful insights about change in general, and especially about "change back" messages.

Chapter Five

WORK AND LIFE

Work can provide a lot of things that we crave, such as a sense of self-worth and importance, a source of friends and social interaction. It helps us to develop our talents and aptitudes and provides a sense of identity. However, most of us think of work only as paid work, our jobs. Unpaid work can also provide these things, but our culture does not encourage us to recognise this, because it has reduced the concept of work to mean paid work only.

Within the world of paid work, there is also a hierarchy of types of work. There is the stimulating, high-status work associated with "career", which provides identity and companionship and a good income. And there are the low-paid, low-status, dead-end jobs that nobody really wants to do, but for which money is seen to be some compensation. Both types have the potential to cause great stress.

On the other hand, because home life can be complicated, time-consuming and unpredictable, and the relationships there often require a lot of attention, the world of paid work is often experienced as a respite from home. It becomes so closely identified with "life work" or career for many people, that the roles involved in it take precedence over the other roles that people take on. Then, they find it difficult to fit those other roles into their schedules.

The paid work ethic also sees jobs as the means by which people are socially included. Employment is considered central to citizenship, in this scheme of things. But many people in high-status, high-paid jobs do not have the time or inclination to do the caring work that builds strong societies. And the low-paid or

those in dead-end jobs are not necessarily genuinely socially included simply by virtue of being employed.

Many — especially older — people wonder why others are
unhappy in their paid work. They are not prepared to shed too
many tears for a high-earning younger generation whose main
problems seem to be "time poverty" and job stress. However, the
world of paid work has changed considerably in recent years.
Brian Thorne points out that we are being taught that life means
"endless toil and competition, the pursuit of ever-greater
achievement, the race for material affluence". Policies directed at
achieving greater efficiency and competition at ever-lower costs
have created a "culture of contempt" that permeates the way we
treat each other in the work- and market-places. Job insecurity
and the spectre of redundancy are always present for individuals
who suffer from their companies' drive for competitiveness.

In the workplace itself, huge effort and commitment are frequently demanded, often beyond what is reasonable, but suppos-
edly justified by high salaries. Projects and teams are often short-
lived, a feature that does not encourage long-term relationships or
commitment. A great deal of routine work is also shift work,
which plays havoc with sleep patterns, health, energy and the
ability to create meaningful relationships outside the workplace.

Time poverty, stress and lives dominated by paid work or lack
of it do not sustain human character, spirit or happiness. Richard
Sennett defines character as the part of the person that involves
long-term emotional experience, loyalty and commitment to others. We are encouraged to be single-minded in pursuit of career
success. This can lead us to compartmentalise our lives and to
deny the ways that the different sections are connected to the
whole and to other people. We are encouraged to ask the question
"who needs me?" only in relation to our paid work. The demands
of much paid work today can set inner, emotional lives adrift,
says Sennett, and with them the sense of self that supports us over
time. We become unable to experience pleasure in simple things,
to prioritise health and happiness. We lose the capacity to inte-
grate the different parts of our lives.

Since the predominant economic conventions do not value unpaid work, they also divide life itself into job and leisure, or work time and "time off". But since the emphasis placed on paid work has meant less time for interpersonal relationships outside the job, many social structures are weak, and leisure is often lonely and boring. Social health suffers, as well as personal health. In a vicious cycle, many people look to their jobs for companionship, stimulation and a structure for their time. As Michael Fogler points out, within this economic model, your life equals your job.

Voluntary Work and Civil Society

Voluntary work in local communities, communities of interest, intentional groups organised around a specific theme or in campaigning groups can provide a great deal of individual satisfaction and reward, while also contributing to the development of a strong civil society. In ancient Greece, Aristotle asserted that the citizen had a duty to obey the law of the state and pay taxes, but that the *good* citizen also played a part in the running of the community.

Voluntary work provides an opportunity for citizens to participate in community decision-making, to make a contribution to the welfare of other people, to get to know other people with common interests, and to feel connected to other people outside their immediate family and friendship groups. It can also help develop skills and knowledge that can be useful in one's paid work or other areas of interest. But voluntary work requires time and all kinds of groups that rely on the unpaid inputs of adults, including credit unions, political parties, sports clubs that rely on adults to coach and organise juniors, parent organisations attached to schools, charitable organisations and community development organisations report difficulties with their activities because of lack of volunteers. Donations of money are often forthcoming, but donations of time are in short supply.

Many of this book's interviewees are involved in voluntary work. Trish Hehir gives time to her local community development association, Richard Douthwaite gives much of his time to Feasta, the Foundation for the Economics of Sustainable Development.

Sheila Ahern and Rose Callan do voluntary work for their children's schools. Anne Louise Gilligan's work for An Cosán is all unpaid. Laragh Neelin is active in the Dublin Food Co-op. They value the work and the contribution it makes to their communities, but they also make time for it. Time is crucial to this kind of work. Money does not compensate for human contact, attention, caring, connection, or passion about ideas and campaigns.

The argument is sometimes made that if money is available through donations, then jobs can be created, and this kind of work can be done by employees of the various organisations. Unfortunately, one danger here is that if donations are not adequate, the employees will have to spend time fund-raising, rather than doing the work that attracted them in the first place. Equally important, doing work that one cares about on a voluntary basis is very different from doing it as an employee. The volunteer is a free agent, who brings this knowledge to the work, but the employee is always constricted by the possibility of disagreement with management or the chance of redundancy.

Visible and Invisible Work

It is not surprising that work has come to mean jobs in today's world. The predominant economic model that influences our society portrays paid work as the only work that contributes to well-being. People who do unpaid work are economically invisible, and they are considered economically inactive. Many activities essential for human happiness are not officially counted as part of the economy. Those who do not have jobs, do not participate in business, or do not accumulate money, including children, retired people, old people, the unemployed, carers in the home, and volunteer workers, are economically invisible.

Work and Gender

Women have traditionally done most economically invisible work. Feminists have long asserted the value of that work, and have opposed the culture that discourages men from identifying as fathers, carers and doers of housework and other domestic tasks. In an egalitarian economy, every adult in a household would mix unpaid caring and domestic work with paid work. Instead, the conventional economic model originally encouraged middle-class men to take their skills into the full-time labour market and to leave women at home to do the unpaid work. Working-class women, by contrast, often did some kind of paid work. Nowadays, the economic model encourages all women to work outside the home, and to pay somebody else to do their caring work. And when women in the paid labour force cannot afford to pay somebody else to do their caring and domestic work, many of them end up doing the "second shift", that is, the bulk of the housework, cooking and childcare, along with their jobs.

Ida Milne and Eoghan Corry (Chapter Seven), Trish Hehir and Micheál Ó Raghallaigh, and Dominic Stevens and Mari-aymone Djeribi (Chapter Eight), currently share the paid and unpaid work in their respective households, questioning both traditional and modern assumptions about work. Bernie Purcell, in *For Our Own Good: Childcare Issues in Ireland*, outlines why such peer relationships are a good way to care for children and to promote gender equality. Barry Jones has chosen to take responsibility for childcare in his family for the time being, while Marcus McCabe and Kate Mullaney have located their business on the same site as their house, so that they can share domestic and business work, although Kate tends to do most of the home-based work. All of these arrangements challenge the traditional view whereby women are considered the only sex properly suited to domestic and caring work. Men, women, children and society at large can only benefit from men's increased identification as fathers, carers and home workers. What is more, many of the interviewees also find that caring and domestic work are complementary to the rest of their work, because during the time they are engaged in such work, the subconscious mind is processing some aspect of their creative or intellectual work.

The traditional devaluation of women's home-based work continues in most parts of society, however. Women who are combining some freelance work with childcare, like Sheila Ahern, Ida Milne and Rose Callan, find that other people's reactions to them are very negative. The fact remains that women who prioritise caring work are seen as boring and dull, even though, as Rose points out, she often is better read and informed than many people who prioritise their jobs to the exclusion of all else.

Life Work

When you did your vision exercises, how did you think about the notion of life work? Work, following a philosophy of enough, is much more than a job. It is anything that gives us satisfaction, recognition or personal growth, or that contributes to the wellbeing of others, or the wellbeing of the planet. Your life work can help you to find out more about yourself, about others and about the world around you. Sometimes, you get paid for it, other times it is not connected to money. The stories below, of Nóirín and of Gearóid Ó Tiarnaigh, show people in the process of exploring their life work.

Nóirín:
Ceramics and Life Work

Nóirín is a ceramic artist and full-time student on a diploma in Ceramic Design and Production. She trained and worked as a nurse for many years, but now considers that her art is her true work. She supports herself with a variety of part-time jobs.

She has lived and worked in America, Germany, England, Australia, New Zealand and Romania. Her nursing allowed her to work periodically, save money and then travel. "I think this is actually the longest period of time that I have been settled. And that has been sheer determination on my part to stay in one country, but also looking at finances and looking at what I want to do myself. I came back in 1992 to educate myself in some fashion or other. I didn't know how I was going to do it, but at this stage, I had decided that I did not want to nurse any more. I loved nursing, I loved communicating with people, but one of the many reasons that I got out of it — there were many — was that I was feeling mental and physical stress and strain. It took me years to get rid of the guilt of saying to myself, no, I do not want to nurse any more, I am not a selfish person for not wanting to nurse any more. I knew then that I had to come back and educate myself in a different way, rethink where I was going."

She did a foundation course at the National College of Industrial Relations, which facilitated access to degree studies at NUI Maynooth, in Anthropology, Ancient Greek and German. Following the degree, she enrolled for an MA in Anthropology. However, she decided not to continue after the first year. She broke her ankle, and the recovery time "threw things into perspective for me in lots of ways. I had to think, I had no alternative but to think. I decided it wasn't worth it. I had got as much as possible out of the subject, and I have no regrets whatsoever for not completing it. I realised that research wasn't necessarily for me. I think it takes a lot of maturity, when one actually realises that, to say, okay, enough is enough." Anthropology, however, remains an important force in her life; she draws on it for her creative work in ceramics, and she explains that "it informs everything I do at the moment".

"Art and the aesthetic awareness of what is in my surroundings has always been a huge part of my life," Nóirín continues. "But the funny thing about it is that I had never really discovered which area of art. And I began to look at different courses that I could do. I started a ceramics class, after I went to live in Cork, and I took to it like a fish to water. That was five years ago, and I haven't stopped making since. Through clay, I have a different method of expressing myself, and it has been a revelation to me. I'm not really able to articulate what I mean in a narrative sense, or in an oral sense. But in a visual sense, I feel that I'm much more in tune with where I'm coming from. I seem to have an affinity with clay, and so I tentatively say, perhaps I have found a niche. I'm not bored with what I'm doing. I can spend large tracts of the day standing, making and feel the time just go — it's gone, and be extremely happy and contented with what I'm doing. And that for me is very, very important.

"I'm as happy as Larry doing that, when essays and seminars don't intervene to interrupt my flow," she laughs. Her BA and MA studies were grant-aided, but her current course is not. "You know, it's tough going. I'm quite happy to finance myself. I have tried to look at jobs very objectively and say, okay, I have to work in order to support myself. I looked at the different types of jobs that I thought would be appropriate, that would not involve a lot of stress, because no matter what I do, I try to put a hundred per cent into it. Otherwise I don't find any point in doing it.

"I could not give a hundred per cent to a job and a hundred per cent to my studies. I've done administrative work with Cork Corporation; I've also done the register of electors for a few years in a row, which I absolutely adore. You meet loads of people. I've worked in call centres, and I have worked in a deli, because I have catering experience also — that kind of thing — they're all means to an end, really." She has resisted opportunities to nurse part-time as a way of earning money. "My studies are a priority. And no matter what job I go to, I point out, in interviews or whatever, that my priority is my study. That is my work. And if they can fit in around my work, well and good. I sound as if I have a choice of jobs; but I have had to look upon my quality of life, because if I am stressed out with my job, I am not going to perform with my ceramics.

"When I'm working, I'm paying back loans, but I'm saving at the same time — always. This has always been part of my life, because of my lifestyle. The Credit Union is fantastic. I avoid banks at all costs. I'm not a gambling-type person. I buy the lotto the odd time, at Christmas or something. Savings — that's the way I exist. My budget is very minimal, and it can be quite stressful not necessarily knowing where the next month's rent comes from. I have developed coping mechanisms and I seem to exist on very little. I'm not materialistic. I don't require designer gear and I don't require the latest in whatever. I rent a TV, which I hardly ever turn on. I use the library for books. I don't run a car, and I have a bicycle. We have a great LETS[1] scheme in Cork and I have bartered some of my pieces. I love cinema and I can go to the cinema. Theatre is wonderful in Cork, I love it, but it can be very expensive. That is one thing that really kills me, that, because of finances, I can't go to the theatre much.

"I live in rented accommodation. I have been *extremely* lucky. I live in the most wonderful maisonette. I'm amazed that it's so cheap, because it's in the centre of Cork. My current flatmate is an artist; he understands perfectly where I'm coming from and we get on extremely well, because we give each other space. I have to be comfortable and secure in my surroundings. I'm good on my own, I've done an awful lot of stuff on my own, but where I live and stay is always very important for me.

"Lots of people think I'm mad. They say, a student once again, Nóirín? Essays! And I tend to agree with them in some ways; I ask myself if I am ever going to stop. But learning has been an integral part of my life, on many levels. Walking up the side of a hill in Thailand and living with tribespeople — it's education; and people thought I was mad then too, but it depends what one's definition of madness is. But once I actually explain to people and they get to know me, they see that there's method in my madness, in lots of ways. And I don't take it on board. I mean, if I did, I wouldn't set foot outside the door, from the very first time I went off to Germany on my own, when I was 17. So it doesn't really make that much difference to me. And my family, my sisters and my brother, have been there for me though thick and thin. They have been supportive of anything that I have done. My partner has also been a very positive force. I'm surrounded by people who love and support me, and that's extremely important."

---

[1] LETS stands for Local Exchange Trading System. It refers to a group of people who agree to trade with each other, but with no exchange of money. See more information in *Resources*.

Gearóid Ó Tiarnaigh:
Healing as Life Work

Gearóid Ó Tiarnaigh joined the Irish Army when he left school, and spent 17 years as an officer before retiring in January 2001 at the age of 35, in order to work full-time as a healer. "It's difficult," he says, "coming from a very organised background, where you have a specific job and it's just so, and people have an understanding of what that is, to just turn around and say, I'm a healer.

"I often describe myself as an intuitive healer. Intuitively, I know what to say to people, or what to do with people, how to deal with certain situations. I work with people and the healing happens, and some of the time I don't know why. And if I trust the knowing in that, it actually works out very well. If I try to control it too much, I find that it doesn't necessarily work so well. I have done courses and trained myself in various disciplines. But there is something more to it than that — it is hard for me to put a finger on it, but I wouldn't consider that it's all down to me. There's more out there than just me; there is a source, for me, there is a God. I'm not a religious person, even though I had a very Catholic upbringing. But I am a spiritual person and I do believe in God.

"I'm coming across a lot of people who are unhappy in their lives, often it's with their jobs, they're stressed out, or they have illnesses because of that situation. And a lot of the time, I just talk to people and reflect things back to them and help them to realise sometimes how they are living to work, and what could they do to change that, and how could I support them in that — give certain skills, use affirmations, use visualisation, things like goal-setting. Most people have a very wishy-washy sense of that; we're never really shown how to do it. Some of that I learned in the army, like goal-setting and management. Other stuff is more a balancing of people's energies, because they're totally out of kilter — their energies are so wrong, that they can't see the wood for the trees. A lot of what I'm doing is not new — it's an ancient healing. Some of the people that come to me have other issues and need to go and see a counsellor or psychotherapist but they don't want to do that, they're not ready for that stage. Somehow, I'm a safe halfway house."

The process of transition from army officer to healer was gradual. "I have changed from the guy I was at 17 or 18 years of age. At 35 or 36, I was a new person, and I was ready to move on. They were difficult choices, because there's a lot of stability in the set-up I was in, there's a lot of security in that, financial and otherwise. And there's a kind of a system there — you just become part of that institution. And it would have been very easy to stay. I was doing well, and I would have been perceived as having ticked all the right boxes, and being on the right career path. I also gained security from it, in that I do have a pension. I would have maximized the pension better by doing maybe 20 or 21 years. But it was important to make the move. A lot of people within the system would have thought I was a bit mad to leave to do what I was doing. I can understand that. In fact, five or ten years ago, *I* would have been that person, shaking my head at someone like that.

"It was a very gradual process and I suppose it's hard to pinpoint specifically. In 1991, I was drawn to do my first massage course, a year-long course in Swedish massage. My biggest interest at that time would have been sports injury, something I could do when I retired from active participation in sports. I went into that at a very academic level — how do the muscles work, and what are the physiological effects. And I wouldn't have seen anything else, non-physiological or holistic, at the time. Maybe I had some sense of it, but I wasn't tuned into that."

In early 1995, Gearóid became ill, experiencing tiredness, lack of energy and dizzy spells. After extensive medical investigations, he was diagnosed with toxoplasmosis and was told that the cure was rest. Over the two years that he suffered from this condition, he began to read about complementary medicine and "eventually, I started to realise that I had my own responsibility in relation to it. I had to decide to get better. I won't call it just positive thinking, but I made a decision that I wanted to get better. I was using some affirmations and I started to believe that I could get better and sure enough, within six months of that, I was right as rain. I went back for tests, and they said I still had it, the medical prognosis was still the same, but something had changed. That was a major eye-opener for me, that there was more to it than the simple, medical, scientific way of treating something."

Gearóid started to do a lot of personal development work at this time. "I started taking more responsibility for who I was and I started doing some psychotherapy because I wanted to get a better sense of myself. I found that a great help, because I found out things about myself that I kind of knew, but kind of didn't know. And that would have been very important to me — understanding myself.

"Over a period of time, I began to realise that the army was no longer for me. But it took me a while to know what I wanted to do. When I was first told that I was a healer, I thought, no way. I thought maybe I could learn a specific skill, like being a therapist, or something in the alternative medical field. But I began to be much more open to different people and different disciplines. Some people that I had started to trust and respect told me that I was a healer and that I had gifts in that area."

Gearóid's wife has supported his changes wholeheartedly. He also believes that many of the couple's financial decisions over the last ten years have facilitated their current choices. "We made some investments which worked out well," he says, adding that coming to terms with financial issues has, nevertheless, been a challenge for him. "We were used to living off two good salaries so there's been a big change, notwithstanding that there's a pension. You're used to living in a certain lifestyle — you have your house, your mortgage, and your normal outgoings, and you're giving up that certain salary. I would have always known exactly how much money we had and how much we were spending and where it was going. And I've had to let go of a lot of control over that, and trust that, if I'm doing the right thing, it actually will be okay. I've gone through periods where things were going well, lots of people were coming, and you're buoyed by that. And then, it's quiet again and I start to question what I am doing. I kept getting drawn back to an old way of measuring myself, by asking how many clients did I have this month, how much money did I make? That's one way to measure how successful I am, instead of asking how am I working as a healer, what's my sense of myself in this, what's the quality of the work that I'm doing? This week could be a good week if I've had two happy clients and next week could be a bad week, if I have ten clients and I get caught in a rut. So all this type of stuff, I'm learning about it as I go along."

He knows that the quiet periods are for "introspection and meditation and getting a better feel for who I am. I had lived my life out of my head, mostly, and there are huge changes for me since I started living out of my body and trusting my intuition and listening to my fears. I'm finding some of those steps difficult. I have my moments when I have no problem with them, and I know that my healing is better when I'm in that better space.

"I have changed my whole view on location. We really love the home we have, but we're not tied down. It's a huge new place for me to be, not to be tied into a specific job. I can go wherever I want and do whatever I want. So, suddenly, having a house in a particular place is not as important as it used to be. And there's a letting go in that. I suppose it's something to do with possessions as well. My older self would have measured myself by my home and my car and my job and my social standing, that I was happily married and all the things on the outside. That has changed a lot.

"For a lot of us, when it comes to change, we are reluctant to change the status quo. We are in a certain place, we have a comfort zone, which I have, which everybody has. I have made steps, but there are still other steps I need to make. Some part of me misses the structure, misses the knowing of a regular job. And that's a challenge for me. When I sit down and journal, or talk with someone of a like mind, I know this is okay, I'm on the right track here. It has been a progression to get to this place, and I definitely don't feel that I'm at a destination. I'm just on a journey, and this is where I'm at, at this moment.

"I sense that at some stage I will write, and down the road, we both have some sort of vision of a healing centre. Really, in twelve months' time, I'm not sure what I'll be doing. It will be related, of course. If I won the lotto in the morning, I'd still be living this life, I would still be on this journey, I'd still be learning who I am, I'd still be healing. That's a really good place to be".

Reaching a Good Definition of Work for You

There are many different ways of defining work, depending on culture, beliefs, values and life experiences. Most of them contradict each other. However, if we break the connection that always links work to money, then we can begin to stop confusing work with paid employment and we can redefine work as any purposeful or productive activity. Paid work becomes just one activity among many and this recognition "frees us from the false assumption that what we do to put food on the table and a roof over our heads should also provide us with our sense of meaning, purpose and fulfilment", according to Joe Dominguez and Vicki Robin. Whether you love or hate your paid employment, it is wise to remember that its purpose is to earn money for necessities. It is not a substitute for the work of being a decent partner, parent, neighbour or friend, or the work of finding expression for one's talents and gifts, or developing a sustaining philosophy of life and learning about yourself and the world.

By separating work from wages, you can find your own definitions of work. "When at your paid job you can value your life energy by working efficiently, diligently, intelligently and for the highest remuneration possible. When doing the rest of your work, you can value your life energy by working efficiently, diligently, intelligently and with the greatest degree of enthusiasm and love you have in you", conclude Dominguez and Robin.

Chapter Six

DEVELOPING FINANCIAL INTELLIGENCE

Money is undoubtedly central to many of the discussions about developing a better life. Yet many of us have never really explored in any detail our attitudes to money and the ways that we use it. Most of us have no financial focus. As with life in general, we are directionless. But we need awareness of the financial choices available to us. This chapter offers a framework and principles for thinking about them. Whether you have a lot of money or a little, it encourages you to use a philosophy of enough to develop your own answers.

Enough is creative. Don't follow the examples and exhortations in this book exhaustively, but use them as encouragement to shape your own life. The process connects time, work and money in a cyclical relationship with each other. If you live within your means, you can control your paid work; that creates more time for all the other kinds of work you want to do. What is more, with time on your hands, you can be creative about living within your means.

Your Money or Your Life

Money is central to the issues of balancing work and time, so that we gain control of our lives. Our understanding of money issues can make or break our plans for balance. A seminal work, and still one of the best, is *Your Money or Your Life: Transforming Your Relationship with Money and Achieving Financial Independence*, by Joe Dominguez and Vicki Robin. The authors offer a definition of money as something for which we exchange our life energy. Working from this definition, they investigate the work–earn– spend cycle of modern economies, and how to break it.

Using the concept of enough, Dominguez and Robin explore how it makes you immune to the pressures of both recession and boom. If you are living well within your means and are not reliant on what many regard as necessary trappings of contemporary life, you won't worry too much when prices become inflated. If the economy goes into recession and your income falls, this way of living will also stand to you. Enough makes you sceptical of the pressures to borrow and spend that happen in a boom, because it puts you in touch with your needs.

Your Money or Your Life is essential reading for every balance-seeker, no matter what their financial situation. It is written in an American context, but its ideas can be adapted for all Western societies. It offers a wealth of ideas on money, consumption, work, and time. It will help you develop financial intelligence and financial integrity, and it also offers a nine-step plan for reaching financial independence. In the meantime, here are some ideas to get you started. Most are adapted from *Your Money or Your Life* and related books, articles and websites.

A Financial Health Check

You can't plan the financial future if you don't know where you are at the moment. You need a clear picture of your finances. The six-step financial check below will ascertain your net financial worth right now. You can do it alone, with a partner or even with older children, depending on your inclinations and relationships. You don't have to do it all at one sitting either, but can do it over a period of time while you assemble all the information. Don't take too much time, though.

Why focus on net worth? As Dominguez and Robin point out, over the years that you have done paid work, from the teenage part-time jobs to wherever you are at the moment, a certain amount of money has entered your life. This exercise examines what you have to show for it. It takes the emphasis off your current income, which is how most people assess themselves financially. The exercise may show that you are deeply in debt or that you are actually financially secure. Now is the time to find out.

1. List all your main assets, such as house, car, motorcycles, boats, bicycles, sports equipment, household goods, clothing, silver, china, jewellery, computers. If you can't remember all the things you own, it is worth literally going around your house, apartment, shed or garage, and taking an inventory. Next to each item, estimate what it would be worth if you sold it. Then list all your savings and investments, including pensions, and their encashment value.

2. List all your liabilities, including outstanding mortgage, loans, money owed on credit cards, unpaid bills and overdrafts, including interest owed.

3. Add up all your assets and all your liabilities, and subtract the liabilities from the assets. This tells you your net worth, in the most simplified, concrete, material sense. You may have a negative net worth, which, according to Dominguez and Robin, is a sobering but not insurmountable state, or you may have a positive one. They go on to point out, however, that *net* worth does not equal *self* worth.

4. Calculate your total net income for a year. Include any investment income, interest from savings, or dividends.

5. List and cost all your outgoings. You will probably find it simple enough to list things like mortgage, rent, repayments on loans, and major purchases such as insurance and fees for various services and utilities. Go on to list all your other outgoings, on food, drink, leisure, motoring, transport, clothing, and so on. Be completely honest about what you spend your money on. Estimate the costs, if you don't keep records, and from now on, start keeping records of everything you spend.

6.   Compare your income with your outgoings. You will be either living well within your means, just about making ends meet, or living outside your means.

Where Are You?

If you are just about making ends meet, or you are deeply in debt, don't despair. Don't blame yourself and don't judge yourself. Just remember that the future starts now. All of the following sections are relevant and will help you get in control of your finances and your life.

If you are financially secure, congratulations. You will find that a lot of what I write is already familiar to you, but you might get some new ideas from it. In my experience, there's always something new to learn.

If you are living within your means, that's good too. It means your income is able to cover the costs of your lifestyle. But ask yourself if you are in an earn-and-spend cycle, where you work hard, spend a lot of money and don't have much time. If this is you, you can probably skip the sections on debt, although you might find some interesting ideas there too, which would increase your assets. You should not skip the sections that encourage you to reflect on whether your spending is in accord with your priorities and values. Nor should you ignore the bits about retail therapy and comfort and competition consumption, because even if you are well able to meet all your expenses, this kind of spending is addictive. It has psychological consequences that are not healthy. It is not conducive to achieving a balanced lifestyle, nor is it good for the planet as a whole.

You could also pay attention to Chapter Nine, *Live Well on Less Money*, which deals with reducing outgoings, as doing so could help you spend even less time at paid work. Think of time as the new wealth, allowing you to pursue your life purpose. At its most crude, consider that time to relax may help your golf, tennis or skiing more than new equipment or expensive lessons. Income is no indicator of wealth, if you are spending everything you earn.

What Are You Spending Your Money On?

A lot of people don't actually know where their money goes. You may take a couple of hundred euros out of the bank on Friday after work, and by Saturday afternoon, it's gone, but you have hardly anything to show for it. Depending on your stage of life and your responsibilities, it could go on alcohol or other drugs, a restaurant meal after work, a take-away meal because you're too tired to cook, swimming and lunch out for your kids, a trip to the garden centre or DIY shop, new clothes, books, CDs or DVDs. Sometimes you buy things that you don't use, or that you use once.

Start Keeping Records

You need to start keeping detailed records of where your money goes. Review them regularly. This will allow you to judge if you are making good use of it, and to plan for future spending.

A good place to start is just to list everything over a few weeks. Then you can divide the expenses into categories like food, transport, leisure, electricity, fuel and so on. You should further divide into sub-categories. For example, under food, you should distinguish between essential basic groceries, comfort food, junk food, food for entertaining at home, restaurant food, take-away food, and any other categories that apply to you. You should also separate out spending that is wholly or mainly connected with your job, such as lunches and coffees at work, clothing, travel and paid childcare.

Doing this exercise over six months, a year, or more will allow you to see patterns in your spending. You will begin to understand where your money goes and what it costs you to live from day to day. You will also be able to estimate how much you spend in a year. You will then be able to make adjustments, depending on how you answer the following questions, as posed by Dominguez and Robin:

- Are your purchases giving you a good return on the life energy that goes into earning the money to buy them? For example, if something costs €100, ask yourself how many hours it took you to earn that net amount, and whether the item is worth that amount of your time and energy.

- Are your purchases in line with your personal values and priorities, which you set out in your vision?

- How many purchases are necessary and how many are just nice to have?

- Could you have got better value for certain items elsewhere, if you had anticipated needing them and had the time to do some research?

- What are your non-reimbursable job-related expenses?

Keeping accurate records is an essential part of working out how much money you actually need to live well, and how much you are spending on things that do not serve you well. It can be a process of self-discovery, as you examine just what proportion of your money goes on necessities and what goes on things that are merely nice to have, or that you don't use very often. This awareness can help you to reduce your outgoings. If you combine this knowledge with the ideas in Chapter Three, on work and life, you will be able to avoid the temptation to work compulsively. You will know when you have earned enough to meet your needs. You also revise your opinion of what constitutes a necessity. The sooner you arrive at your personal definition of enough, the more freedom you will have to explore alternative ways to work, and to create time in your life.

How Much Does Your Job Cost You?

Most of us know our net income, that is, what is left in our pockets after tax and other deductions have been made. But many fail to take into account the other job-related expenses that eat into take-home pay. It has become a bit more common in recent years to cite the cost of childcare, but what about job-related clothing, the cost of a car to get to work, the lunchtime shopping that you do only because you are on a break from your job and the opportunity is there, the coffees and lunches out, the collections for gifts and other social occasions? Many people "treat" themselves when work is taxing or boring, thus adding to the "need" to earn even more. You can probably add to the list.

The costs of your job should be deducted from your net income, after tax. If your job is leading you into an exhausting work–earn–spend cycle, then you have little to show for your investment of life energy.

What Other Ways Do You Spend?

Are you spending for comfort?

Job-related stress and exhaustion lead to spending pressures — massage, therapy, including "retail therapy", convenience food, comfort foods, cleaning services, frequent hotel or resort breaks. If you weren't working as you do, you could reduce or eliminate many of these pressures. Money can bring temporary relief from them, but it really is only temporary. Moreover, retail therapy is addictive and a problem, even if you are able to easily cover the bills.

Where are you spending competitively?

Competitive patterns of consumption emerge when we want to be better than the next person and want to show it by virtue of our clothes, shoes, cars, holidays, houses and furnishings. Our hunger for material possessions can be a symbol of unmet emotional needs for status and security. Our culture encourages us to be competitive about status. If we want to prove our earning power or our sexual success, we are encouraged to buy certain types of cars. Many of us are looking for the ultimate holiday destination, where none of our friends or colleagues has been. We tend to attribute this kind of buying to others and deny it in ourselves. Be completely honest with yourself as you reflect on your spending in this light.

Are you establishing an identity by means of your spending and possessions?

Competitive spending is also linked to a feeling that our possessions express who we are. Are your spending patterns linked to your social identity? How do you judge yourself? I am not claiming that we all purchase to create an identity and to establish our status. But we do compare our lifestyles with others. Who is in your reference group? What statements do you make about yourself, by means of your possessions?

Are you spending defensively?

Many parents spend defensively for their children, buying them the "right" clothes so that they won't be conspicuous at school and in social situations. Do your children and their friends expect to be entertained by a professional at birthday parties, instead of entertaining themselves or participating in games that you organise? Have you given in to the pressures to hire a magician or arrange an outing, because that is fast becoming the norm? Are you spending on the most up-to-date computers or on fee-paying schools, fearful that your children will be left behind in the job and education market? Do you buy things for your children in order to compensate for the fact that you spend long periods of time apart, while you are at work?

What are you planning to spend money on in the future?

Our consumerist culture teaches us to judge ourselves and prove our worth through the things we *possess*. If we are not happy, content or balanced, it is because we haven't found the correct things, or can't afford them. Wellbeing then comes from sources outside ourselves, and what we don't have. Are you planning to buy a new computer, install a new kitchen, or a new deck in your garden? Will you have the time to use them? What do you really want? Do you want to relax in the garden, but won't have the time if you have to work to pay for the deck? Do you want to cook more and share meals with friends and family? Will you have any friends left to come to dinner, or even the time and energy to cook for them, by the time you pay for the new kitchen? Do you really need a restaurant-standard stainless steel cooker, in order to produce an enjoyable meal? Do you want to achieve a work or study goal by having a faster, more up-to-date computer? Will it really help you to achieve the goal? If you look at the fantasy or the dream underlying the desire for the new possession, could you actually achieve the dream without the possession?

Is Your Consumption in line with Your Personal Values?

The conventional way of thinking about economics tells us that earn-and-spend is good, and that we should buy ever-more possessions in order to "keep the economy going" and keep GNP growing. Or, if the economic bubble bursts and recession sets in, we are asked to "tighten our belts".

How does earn-and-spend square with most people's desire for a clean environment? The more things we have, the more of the earth's resources are used up in manufacturing them. The four-wheel-drive car is advertised as providing freedom from city life, and access to places "away from it all". But is it really a chance to get closer to nature and peace, or is it a polluting commodity that degrades rural terrain, as well as being a leading cause of accidental death? Which do you value most?

Do you really want to support brands that are made desirable through advertising, but which are designed to hook lower-income young people into wanting products that their parents cannot afford? Juliet Schor asks us to consider whether Nike really wants to empower women, as the company's ads suggest, considering that it pays $1.60 a day to female Vietnamese workers. And many other brand manufacturers are equally exploitative of workers.

With increasing consumption, lower-income children and adults are left behind in the market, and the gap between the affluent and the poor becomes unbridgeable, Schor continues. This results in gated communities, who try to protect themselves from

the poor outside by means of increased security. (On a global
level, states similarly try to protect themselves from economic
refugees who leave countries that have been bypassed in the
global market, as has almost the entire continent of Africa, except
for South Africa.) And as the pressures on private spending grow,
support for taxes and public spending goes down. Public facilities
get little support, they deteriorate, and because they are not of a
good standard, pressures increase to spend on private facilities.

Do these aspects of consumption fit in with the things you
want for yourself, your community and your planet, which you
identified in your personal vision (see Chapter Two)?

"I Have No Choice"

A common reaction to these observations is to deny that one has a
choice when it comes to spending in today's world. We assert that
survival in the rat race demands certain kinds of spending. Many
of us believe that we truly need a range of products that Juliet
Schor calls the "new essentials", from the latest in mobile phones
to bottled water.

Consumerist culture promotes a continual blurring of the dis-
tinctions between the possessions we need and the possessions we
want. The result is to make us believe that we have no choice but
to spend in line with this culture. But the culture is one of over-
spending, often spending more than we realise and frequently
spending beyond our means, using credit cards and often accru-
ing debt. Juliet Schor's American study found that the single biggest reason for staying in a frantic lifestyle was personal debt.

Are You in Debt?

If there is anything that comes close to a financial rule for balanced living, it is: keep debt to a minimum. Debt results in worry
and poor mental health. Getting out of it is liberating.

All of the people who feature in this book are guided by some
version of this principle. Some view mortgages as debts to be
avoided and have done so throughout their lives. Others have

cleared their mortgages, using lump sums gained on redundancy or early retirement. Still others are prepared to have small mortgages, making sure they don't buy more house than they can afford, while keeping clear of other long-term debt. This may sometimes mean doing without, waiting to do home improvements, or living in rented accommodation, but it means they do not overstretch themselves financially. When borrowing seems like the best option to finance a plan, they tend to use their Credit Union rather than banks. They all avoid credit card debt. When they use credit cards, they pay off the amount owed in full at the end of the month. They save for purchases and pay cash when they can.

The issues are different, of course, for people who are balancing their lives with sufficient financial resources, and those who are struggling with severe debt. If you are seriously in debt, you need to draw up a firm plan for getting out of it. You may be able to do this alone, but you could also go to your local Money Advice and Budgeting Service, which is free to all citizens. I would also strongly advise you to follow the plan in the book *Your Money or Your Life*. Below are some other suggestions.

- Could you reduce your material needs and wants, and thus your outgoings, by 15–20 per cent of your after-tax income, and use the money saved to pay off your debts? See Chapter Nine for ideas on reducing outgoings.

- Can you earn extra money to use for the sole purpose of paying off your debts? For both of the above options, you should set up electronic or direct debit methods of payment that ensure the money goes to pay off the debt. If you don't, unless you are exceptionally strong-willed, you will be tempted to spend it. When the debts are paid off, you can work less, or you can do the same amount of work and save for a while. You will be used to living well within your means. But don't let paid work become the dominant feature of your life.

- Consider selling your car and using the money from the sale, as well as the savings on running costs, to clear some debt.

The costs of car ownership are huge, particularly if part of your debt was acquired to buy the car in the first place.

- Do you have any other assets that you could realise, in order to clear some of your liabilities? Some of the ways to sell material goods are through second-hand shops, car boot sales and *Buy and Sell* magazine.

- Get rid of credit cards when you are in debt. If you must have a card, get a charge card (see below).

- Consider renting out a room, if you are a home-owner.

- Once you have cleared your debts, do everything you can to avoid debt in the future.

People often assume that there is no alternative to assuming substantial debts at a certain stage of life. Get into the habit of questioning assumptions like these and examining creative alternatives. In order to avoid debt, learn to understand money. Understand that when you buy on credit and defer payment, you may end up paying several times the price of the goods. It is financially wise to avoid as much debt as possible from early in life.

Credit Cards

Credit cards make the cost of purchases seem less real than when you use cash. Because you don't have to pay off the debt completely each month, it is easy for debt to get out of hand. If you are in debt, you should get rid of all credit cards, as recommended in the previous section. If you are not in debt and you currently have more than one card, you should get rid of all but one. Use it only when you have the money to pay off debt in full at the end of the month. Be disciplined about clearing the full debt.

Ideally, you should pay cash for purchases, because it is easier to keep track of spending, and the money seems more "real". If you must use a card, consider a charge card, on which you must pay off the entire balance each month.

Saving

Living within your means is the first and most important step to becoming financially secure. A second step is to pay yourself from within those means, so that you have money available to you for both short-term and long-term security. Saving can have different purposes. It can provide a cushion equivalent to a few months' income, in case you are not able to earn. Savings can be used to make cash purchases for big items such as dental repairs, holidays and cars, thus avoiding debt. Savings can also be invested, in order to provide for a time when you will not do any more paid work.

Saving for the short term

There is great peace of mind to be found in having a cushion of savings put by, which you can draw on to cover monthly expenses if you don't get paid for freelance work or if you are made redundant. Conventional financial advice usually recommends savings to the value of three months' income. It is really up to you to decide how much is appropriate, depending on your ability to live within your means, and the number of debts you have to service. It is clearly an advantage to have little or no debt, as this will mean your savings will go further if you have to use them to cover regular monthly expenses.

You may also decide to have a separate saving fund for one-off purchases like computers, cars and holidays, or in case an emergency requires you to spend money on travel or some other intervention. Dental expenses and medical bills can often arise when you least expect them and it is very satisfying not to have to go into debt to meet them. Purchases like a new winter coat or shoes can also strain the monthly budget, and knowing that you can buy from savings helps avoid the temptation to buy on credit.

Depending on circumstances, you could even build a house from savings, thus avoiding a mortgage. Marcus McCabe and Kate Mullaney, who feature in Chapter Eight, built their house in instalments, waiting each time until they had enough money saved.

Even if you cannot avoid a mortgage altogether, the more money you save towards buying a house, the better off you will be.

Saving for any kind of large purchase demands delayed gratification. It may also mean buying a modest house or apartment, or a second-hand car. It means making do without, while saving for the purchase. In short, saving demands self-discipline.

Saving for the long term

Another way to save is to invest money for children's future education or for your own retirement. If you are in paid employment, you may have a pension plan available through your employer. If not, or if you have additional funds set aside in a savings plan for retirement, you need to learn to understand the investment market. If you are planning to leave paid employment in the future, or to work part-time in your job, you could investigate making Additional Voluntary Contributions (AVCs) now, while you have the extra income.

Not everybody considers savings and investments to be the best option for the future. It can be difficult to ensure that one's money is ethically invested; investment makes its own contribution to economic growth, and the stock market can collapse at any time. It can be argued that the best way to provide security in the future is to work towards creating a caring society — something we can do only if we have time to invest in other people.

The rent from property can create both current and future income, as in the case of Laragh Neelin, whose story is in Chapter Eight. Laragh was lucky enough to inherit property. Her ability to live well on a small income, combined with the rent from rooms in her two homes, which she is careful to rent in non-exploitative ways, gives her adequate security. Richard Douthwaite, who also tells his story in Chapter Eight, has no long-term savings but lives within an extended family that offers long-term support. Portfolio workers (see Chapter Four), a description that fits Richard, are also able to do paid work in manageable ways beyond the usual retirement age, because of the flexible nature of their work arrangements.

If you decide to save for the long term, the earlier you start the better, to take advantage of compound interest. But it is never too late. Low-risk investments with modest but sure returns are best for people working within a philosophy of enough. Think carefully about the amount of income your child's education will take or that you will require when you eventually cannot do paid work. How much do you really need? Is your estimation based on current lifestyle? If you start living a more balanced life, if you cut your expenses, prioritise quality of life, rather than standard of living, if you avoid debt and are able to live without waste and within your means, and if your children are able to do the same, then you won't need the vast sums that many people caught up in the earn-and-spend culture consider necessary.

Do your own homework, and don't depend completely on experts for advice. Use good books, like *Family Finance* by Colm Rapple, to get started. For assistance, you could consult an independent financial planner who charges by the hour, instead of relying on commission. Many financial planners and stock brokers want you to believe that investing is complicated, so that you will pay them for their expertise. Choose a consultant carefully, preferably on a recommendation from someone you trust. Learn to understand pensions, investment and the related tax system, so that you can make the best possible use of the knowledge of the experts, when you do consult them.

Pay yourself first

Whatever your reasons for saving, a very good principle for regular saving is to pay yourself first. If you have regular monthly income, have the money come out of your income, either at source, if you are salaried, or via a monthly direct debit if you use a bank account. That way, there is no temptation to spend it. If you get paid irregularly, you need to ensure that your savings schemes are included in your calculations for using the money, and that the schemes themselves are flexible, to allow you to deposit lump sums when you have money.

Money and the Bigger Economic Picture

Making money is the basis of our present economy. People use their life energy to make money by means of business, buying and selling goods and services, and doing other paid work. Money is seen as the primary source of society's wealth and wellbeing, and making money is integral to the concept of economic growth.

Growth is concerned with raising productivity, increasing competitiveness, developing new markets, increasing employment, stimulating investment and encouraging consumer confidence so that people spend more. This view tells us that economic growth should take precedence over all other considerations, and that the rest of life — people in their homes, families, communities, unpaid work, government, education, art, culture, religion and spirituality — is dependent on the economy for wealth and well-being. It is assumed that economic growth will bring about progress for everybody, usually understood as individual betterment and material enrichment.

In this view, the most widely accepted indices of wellbeing are gross national product (GNP) and gross domestic product (GDP). In Ireland, GNP is the more appropriate one, because we have so many multi-national corporations, who repatriate their profits. GNP is the total amount of money spent in a year by a country's consumers on all goods and services. The GNP *per capita* (per head) is the GNP divided by the population; it is the money value of all the goods and services that pass through the life of an average person in a year, including food, clothing, medical bills, fees for services, and a person's share of public service salaries. It also includes the cost of activities such as public tribunals.

GNP takes into account only the aspects of life that can be measured in money terms. If you grow your own vegetables, instead of buying them, the GNP goes down, even though your quality of life may go up. Incidents like car accidents increase GNP, because they increase spending on hospital expenses, repair bills, car purchases and insurance premiums. A pollution incident increases it, because the clean-up has to be paid for.

The GNP *per capita* measure does not tell us how goods are distributed throughout the population. Some families may have two houses, while others have none. You're working harder and longer hours, so you buy more take-away meals and more convenience food at the supermarket. Again, GNP goes up, but it is no indicator of wellbeing, as pointed out by Richard Douthwaite.

After a certain point, increasing wealth does not bring increasing happiness. In fact, living in an age of wealth and in a high-tech economy is the cause of extreme stress. We may become rich in material possessions, and this is often cited as evidence that we have a high standard of living, but we become poor in time. Social relationships suffer, and everybody's quality of life disimproves. Not only that, but the activities that create money do not take into account other systems, such as family, social cohesion, the environment, or fragile eco-systems.

Most Western governments are keen for GNP to grow, and use it as an indicator of improving conditions, but many alternative economists and systems thinkers, including Hazel Henderson, Herman Daly, Richard Douthwaite and Barbara Brandt, say we should use different indices, such as the Index of Social Health, or the Genuine Progress Indicator, or the Index of Sustainable Economic Welfare. The things that are important in these indices include working conditions, environmental quality, fair distribution of income, levels of health, quality of housing, levels of cultural and spiritual activity, standard of education, and time *not* spent in paid work. The government of Bhutan has introduced the concept of Gross National Happiness (GNH) as an indicator of a nation's progress.

You can make your own choices about what indicators to use, in order to assess quality of life. A national shift in priorities will arise only out of the choices you and I make and out of the creative experiments we are prepared to put into practice in our lives.

Chapter Seven

OUT OF THE RAT RACE AND INTO LIFE: DOWNSHIFTERS TELL THEIR STORIES

This chapter tells, mostly in their own words, the stories of five people who have left the rat race behind. Some experienced distinct turning points, such as personal illness or the illness of a friend. Others reached their decisions more gradually. They are clear about the benefits of the choices they have made and are aware that they were fortunate to have the cushion of redundancy lump sums or retirement gratuities, in all but one case. They are also frank about the downsides of their choices and the worries that they sometimes have about their futures.

એ એ એ

Ida Milne and Eoghan Corry: Creating Time

When I visited Ida Milne and Eoghan Corry on a weekday afternoon, Eoghan was out, as he was taking their six-year-old daughter Síofra to her ballet class. Contrast this with the time when they left home at seven in the morning, taking Síofra and their older daughter, Connie (now 10), to the babyminder. Later, Connie would take the school bus from her minder's house, and after school, would go back to her minder's on the bus. Once, she was so tired that she fell asleep on the bus and didn't get off at the correct stop, causing a panic for the minder and Eoghan and Ida, until the driver found her when he finished the run. Eventually, the whole family would get home at seven in the evening. "Everything was pretty well highly strung," says Eoghan. "And if anything went wrong — a cough or the slightest cold — disaster." "As soon as they got a cold or anything, they were straight to the doctor," adds Ida, "packed with antibiotics or whatever, because they just had to get well quickly. They hadn't the two or three days comfort that it might take."

Ida and Eoghan now work from home. These days, the children wake up in their own time and are taken to school by a relaxed parent. The only one who gets up really early is Eoghan, who often rises at four, to work uninterrupted until the children are ready for school. The girls are rarely ill now, and when they are, they don't have antibiotics. "You put them to bed and give them a hot water bottle and feed them oranges and chocolate," Ida adds. Indeed, sometimes, sick children from neighbouring families come and spend a day on their sofa while their parents are at work.

Both Ida and Eoghan are in their early forties. Until 1997, they both held demanding jobs with national newspapers for over 15 years, Eoghan as a journalist and Ida as a librarian. They took the decision to work from home primarily so that they could be with their children more. Eoghan was the first to take the plunge. He had differences of opinion with his management and "resigned in a huff", as he puts it. However, he had been considering leaving for some time before that, and had taken on a freelance contract, which saw him through the immediate post-resignation time. He had also written books, which generated self-employed income, so he knew how the tax system worked. "It can be traumatic when somebody moves from PAYE," he says, "but I'd already done that. I could see the advantages and the disadvantages." The strain on their lifestyle had also been taking its toll on Ida's health and when a redundancy offer was made a few months later, she accepted it. Around the same time, they were building their house in rural Kildare, and designed it with a home office and all the communications technology that they need to carry on a professional journalism career. Eoghan produces all the material and Ida provides editing, design and other support.

Eoghan feels that they have not really scaled down since they both gave up their jobs. They live well, and run two cars. But they are careful with their money; they don't make purchases without considerable thought, they pay cash whenever possible and they clear all credit card debt each month. Their only outstanding debt is a mortgage. "What you don't do easily is take on extra debt, the debt that you service monthly, which PAYE workers will tend to do," says Eoghan. "They will pay for a computer on instalments, whereas we do the opposite, we try and save, try and get a month when we can put our two-and-a-half thousand in the bank for the computer, and then it's done. It's empowerment, it's control. You feel if you really need £5,000[2], you actually have the capacity to get it. Whether that will be true in the next while, I don't know. But we always do believe that you can scale it down if you need to." Ida also says that their work-related expenses are lower. They don't need to buy and maintain office-style clothing any more, nor does she have expensive haircuts. As well as that, "We don't have a hundred and something pounds a week to spend on a baby minder; we don't have fifty pounds a week to spend on travelling or lunches out. You're less likely to stop at the Chinese on your way home."

Ida got a redundancy lump sum, which they put away as a "peace-of-mind fund". She says she would have found it very difficult to give up her job without that. Although she works with Eoghan, she doesn't actually get paid from the contracts and they are both aware of the difficulties that can arise if the non-earning partner has no discretionary money. They have thus "corralled" one source of income that goes straight to Ida's personal account.

The lump sum is slowly diminishing, as they dip into it for various reasons, such as when Eoghan did not get paid for

---

[2] Most of the interviews in this book were conducted before the euro changeover.

a piece of work in 2000. He has developed strategies for coping with the uncertainty of freelance work. One is to always have a column in a national publication, no matter how badly paid, in order to keep a national profile. "It's completely for advertising purposes," he says. He always tries to have at least one project that will pay on time. He also maintains a diversity of contracts. "I do some PR, some trade magazines, some national publications, edit a couple of magazines and I have been involved in the setting up of television programmes. So you're always aware that you can turn your hand to anything," he explains. He has found that "diversity is good, but at the same time, you have to tack down a couple of areas of specialism, so that people come to you for that". His own specialism is sports history. For a couple of years, he also did some teaching on a master's degree in journalism, but "that had its downsides, such as the commuting. It's not a good idea to be tied down on particular days when you're working freelance," he says, "particularly if you need to travel. You probably can get away, if you juggle things round, but there's an added stress there."

They considered moving to the west or southwest of Ireland, when they first went freelance. Now, though, they are very glad that they stayed within commuting distance of Dublin. "You really need to be close to the city, you have to be at functions, you have to be close to your contacts," says Eoghan. If he misses anything about his previous posts, it's the opportunity to exchange ideas with colleagues, "When a topic comes up and you kick it around with five or six people in the office, it works things through your head a lot quicker than it would if you were just doing it yourself. The sparking of ideas and good lines is very important."

They say that many friends find it difficult to accept their choices. "You talk about staying at home, and the children, and they do get upset, particularly people with children. It makes them feel guilty, I think," says Eoghan. "It's something you don't actually bring up very much. It sounds like you're boasting about it, about how happy we are, and how empowered we are." Ida adds, "You actually get people shouting at you. They always say, oh, of course you can do that, we'd love to do that but we couldn't. They think that our mortgage is lower or that we must have got an inheritance somewhere or that something makes us different." She also finds that women in particular often get angry with her for giving up her job: "A lot of them sort of feel I've let the sisterhood down." Nevertheless, some friends, especially those with children, have talked to them and made changes in their working patterns as a result.

Ironically, many of their journalist friends think that it's too difficult for journalists to work from home, while other friends think that Ida and Eoghan can do it because they are journalists. Eoghan thinks that most people working for newspapers could do a large amount of work from home, even without going freelance, "But the newspapers won't accept it. It's interesting that it never happened. And it's not just newspapers. In other jobs, I think a lot of people are commuting to work who don't need to. But of all the professions, we can do it. The problem is we have just sat there, as a profession, sort of waiting for it to happen, and it never did."

Eoghan says that he is probably more obsessed with work now than he was when he held salaried positions, because of the precarious nature of the freelance world. He says it's very stressful to know that it's possible that he won't find work or won't be paid. Nevertheless, he is certain that he has done what is best for him and his family. "The benefits were immediate," he says. "Even if I had just come home and said I'd given up work, without planning it, the benefits were so enormous that it would have worked." He loves being available for his children, being free to take them to school or to spend time with them on other activities. The positive effects on the children have been "massive", he says. "They were tired all the time, their rules were the baby-minder's rules, not ours," Ida adds. "We had literally worn ourselves out."

The thing they enjoy most about their lifestyle is having time. The household has a relaxed and welcoming feel. There is time to be a better friend and neighbour than before. They know a lot more people in their local area now, because they shop locally and are often out and about. "Before, we were just coming and going to the house, and all our contact was in the work situation," says Eoghan. They rarely go out socially, because Eoghan goes to bed early in order to rise at four, but they love to have people visit. "People call by, because they know we're nearly always here," says Ida. She has time to study for an open learning degree in history. Each one has time to travel separately, with or without the children. "I don't have to negotiate my days off, to coincide with his. I've just been away for eight days with my mother, which just wouldn't have been possible before," says Ida. They would both make the same choices again, and their only regret is that they didn't make the changes earlier. Although they are aware of the risks involved in working freelance, they are adamant: "We *are* happy with it, we wake up every morning and thank God for it."

⇛ ⇛ ⇛

Henry McGeeney:
Learning to Let Go

Henry McGeeney gave up a job as a management accountant in 1997, when he was 50, and now makes a living working four days a week in alternative therapies. He practises reflexology, kinesiology, massage, and herbal medicine, testing for microbes, allergies etc., from his home in suburban Kildare. He was an accountant for almost 30 years, and in management for the last 19. Of his last company, he says, "It was always a great place, but also a very busy place to work, and as the years went on, there was more and more responsibility being put on me. Thirteen years ago, I got a diploma in reflexology and I was beginning to practise a bit from home at night time. And then I did a massage course followed by many kinesiology courses. I was always doing courses in alternative therapies. Coming up to 1997, this — treating people from home — was beginning to look very attractive to me while the stress of the existing job was such that I was thinking I needed a change.

"The work was building up, and it was so difficult to get things done. You were always going to meetings. And the commuting time was increasing — when I started in the company first, I'd be at work in 15 to 20 minutes. By the time I left, 19 years later, it was taking three-quarters of an hour to get there. It was actually agonising at that time as to whether I should go or stay, because the pay was good, I had a company car, a pension scheme, my health insurance was paid, and I had many other perks. The change was going to mean less pay while having to pay extra bills."

Coming up to the time he left the company, Henry struggled to keep going. "What I'm doing now was looking very, very attractive and what I was doing with the company was becoming very, very stressful and difficult. It was kind of looking black," he says. He and Jeanne, his wife, went on holiday to France and, away from the stresses of the job, decided that he would take the plunge and hand in his notice, which he did on his return.

"All the managers in the parent company said I was mad, making a big mistake giving up the job," continues Henry. He feels that he couldn't have done it without the continued support of Jeanne, and his daughters, Sinéad and Deirdre, who were 17 and 19 at the time. Jeanne is a teacher, and they both feel that the decision would have been more difficult if she hadn't had an income. Other friends and relations were also supportive. "Some of them were kind of stunned alright," says Henry, "but I've never had a bad reaction from them." He had to give three months' notice and during that period he started building up a clientele for the time when he would be a full-time therapist.

He left with a small lump sum, which he used to pay off his mortgage and do some home improvements. He was keen not to have any debts. His main financial worry was the education of his daughters. "They were of college-going age, which in a way is the most expensive time. Initially, we thought we'd have to make more cutbacks than we did. But then, I have never had a bad day at this work. But we're not extravagant — we're comfortable, but not extravagant."

Henry has a very active spiritual life and believes that people are guided towards what is right for them. "It's funny, how you find the things you need. We were on holidays in Sligo in 1979, and Jeanne got talking to a woman who became my guide and mentor — she introduced me to reflexology and was always more than willing to help me and advise me."

In the beginning, like a lot of freelance workers, he worried that he would not get enough work to cover his budget, and tended to take on too much work. Now, however, he has reached a more comfortable stage. "You go through stages where you say, God, I hope I'm going to have enough people today. And then you get to a stage where you feel comfortable. My diary is always full, which is great — I have a waiting list. But for some reason, you won't get anybody ringing you for a week. And then the next week the phone never stops. That doesn't bother me anymore, but there was a time when it did."

Two years into the change, Henry decided to work only four days a week. "I made the decision that I wasn't going to work Wednesdays any more. So now — I'm kind of thinking — can I take another day off? We'd also like to think that Jeanne could job-share within a short time — we'd have enough to be comfortable. We may eventually sell our house and get somewhere smaller — cosy and easy to run." He loves working only four days: "I really enjoy my days off, you know," he laughs.

Henry still works "pretty hard" on the days he sees clients. "I love talking to people — and this is people really relating their fears and their problems, emotions and so on. I actually think you're very close to nature and God when you're working in this line, because you're striving to help people. It's great; I love working on a one-to-one basis. It can be very rewarding, although it can be very draining some-times." He and another local practitioner treat each other on a reciprocal basis and he is part of a network of practitioners who support each other. He also staggers his hours, taking time out to meditate, walk or play golf in the afternoons, and seeing some clients in the evenings. He also tries not to cluster his more draining cases.

The work is very much a part of his life and although he plans to cut down on the amount he does, he sees himself continuing it indefinitely. "For a start, it gives you a focus. And as well as that, it actually is very, very exciting. Because when you're testing someone, it's as if something else comes into play. It's magical at times. There's intuition there as well. You're trying to read the situation with a client and all of a sudden, something will come into your head and you test it and — oh, that's it!"

He doesn't feel isolated by working at home, because he's meeting people all the time. "I actually think that leaving the company was a letting go. The only thing I regret slightly is that I didn't leave sooner. I always say to my daughters, don't stay too long in one job; move around, get experience. I got into accountancy by default. I suppose I didn't know what I wanted to do, but I got one honour in the Leaving Cert, and you could get into accountancy with that, at that time. Al-though I enjoyed the time I spent at accountancy, I should have left sooner. In letting it all go, I've gained an awful lot of wealth. By wealth, I don't mean physical wealth. The work I do now definitely creates job satisfaction. And I always feel I'm on the right road. I remember, when I left, there was a small do and I was sitting beside the boss' wife and she said, 'You're going out on your own, to find yourself, aren't you?' And that was exactly what I was doing. I feel happy that I've made the right decision in following a career that holds a great interest and deep fascination for me."

ॐ ॐ ॐ

Sheila Ahern:
Leaving Frenzy Behind

Sheila Ahern is 42 and lives with her partner and their two sons, Oscar (5) and Finn (7), in west Dublin. In September 2000, she took voluntary redundancy from her job as a production assistant/researcher with RTÉ, where she had worked for twelve years. Sheila is now doing some freelance work from her home.

She describes winter mornings when she was in her job, getting the children ready to leave, driving them to crèche and school, before going to her own workplace. "I was always rushing the children along, hurrying them up getting their breakfast and getting dressed. Sometimes we'd be sitting here in the kitchen and you could see the headlights from the traffic outside the door, in the pitch dark, the cars were backed up at half seven in the morning. I wouldn't have time for breakfast and would end up drinking coffee in the car. I'd have to try and force the kids to eat, and Oscar would say, 'But it's night time, I'm tired, I want to go to sleep.' They were so young, standing here in the pitch dark in their jammies, looking at me. We'd get into the car at eight o'clock, first to Cabra to the crèche, then to Glasnevin to the school, then to Donnybrook by about half nine. So it was an hour and a half in the car.

"I know it's kind of clichéd, but the traffic was I think the one thing that tipped me over the edge in terms of making a decision to leave full-time employment. Sitting in the traffic thinking, I'm going to be late. Meanwhile, back at home the washing machine is packed with damp clothes and hasn't been emptied for days, the laundry going dirty in the machine and needing to be re-washed. You know, there was just so much rushing around — it was madness.

"Frequently at lunchtime, I'd dash out to the supermarket to get some food for the dinner. I had about three childminders for Finn, different people picking him up from different places, to eventually drop him to my father's house. I would pick them both up from my Dad's house and get home here at about seven in the evening with the Weetabix from breakfast time now congealed on the table. If you ever want a good builder's material, I highly recommend Weetabix. Trying to scrape the Weetabix off the table and get food ready for dinner with two tired children and clean up the mess in the house was not an easy task.

"We had some great people helping look after the children, but if one got sick, or if a child was sick, you would be under terrible pressure. I remember one of the children being sick in the middle of the night and wondering, will he be all right by nine o'clock or am I going to have to take the day off? Will he stop vomiting in time to take him to the crèche? Will the crèche know that he's been sick during the night and think I'm a negligent parent because I'm sending him in when he's ill? Or if I dose him with Calpol, will he be all right? No matter how flexible an employer is, if you have a fixed schedule of commitments for the day it is very difficult to change at short notice. There can also be conflict between the parents: my day is more important today than yours. I can't get out of what I'm doing today, you can. What would often happen was that I would cancel work and bring the child to the doctor and half an hour later the child would be laughing and playing and not a bother on them.

"The worst point came when Oscar said to me one morning, 'Are you sad?' He was only two years old at the time and he was asking me was I sad. I said, 'No, of course I'm not sad.' But it dawned on me that, with this whole lifestyle, I just wasn't happy. I was getting by, and ploughing from day to day, and week to week. Even when planning holidays — I would think about 'getting through' Christmas. And everything was, 'Now, if we get through this, and we get through that, and then we only have six months before the next major hurdle.' You shouldn't be 'getting through' Christmas, you should be enjoying yourself. I want to enjoy my life now and not some time in the distant future."

Sheila thinks that she nevertheless would probably have kept going like this, had she not become ill. "It just got to me eventually and it was very dramatic. I thought I was having a heart attack and I ended up in the Mater Hospital, in the Emergency Department." The project she was working on at that particular time was extremely demanding. "It was very intense work on all levels involving a huge time and emotional commitment. I started getting panic attacks. I couldn't understand it. I felt like I was in total control, because I was able to get on and do my job and do it well. For all intents and purposes, I looked fine and seemed to be perfectly normal.

"When you talk about stress, you think of being under pressure, nobody likes it; it's not very nice. But I had no concept that it would have such a physical effect — I'd wake up in the morning, and the first thing I would do was get sick. I couldn't understand why I was vomiting a lot, why I had headaches and couldn't sleep. So I presumed it had to be a physical cause. And it continued for quite a long time. I am lucky to have a very good GP who took it all very seriously." Sheila eventually had lots of tests that proved there was nothing wrong with her heart, but she was reluctant to accept this diagnosis. "I kept saying, it's not in my head, it's not in my head, it's in my chest, don't tell me this is psychological, it's physical."

Currently, Sheila and Kevin are free of mortgage and childcare costs. "We were paying £700 a month childcare, after tax, at one stage. You step out of that when they go to school, to some extent, but then you've got after-school care if you can get it." I sensed the stress and near panic again as she described the difficulty of getting good childcare. "Even if you can get childcare, it needs to be extremely flexible as the school has quite a lot of days off as well as half days, mid-term breaks and long Christmas and summer holidays. The strain of that when you are working full-time is dreadful. To find somebody now who would pick them up after school and take care of them until I got home from work would be almost impossible.

"I am determined not to take on freelance work that is not worth the time and effort involved. I'm very lucky to be in this position in a time when there are plenty of jobs around; to some extent I can pick and choose the type of work I want to do. I work from home and can make full use of technology in the form of the Internet and e-mail, which saves so much time and effort."

Even when she was working full time, Sheila avoided debt, apart from a mortgage. She attributes a reluctance to get into debt to her background. "My parents both left school at 12 or 13 and my father has always had a real fear of getting into debt. I suppose it comes from growing up in the 1940s and '50s, when he saw the effects being indebted to money-lenders had on families. His attitude was that you do not borrow money. A mortgage, okay, but you do not borrow money."

Since Sheila has always had a careful approach to money and borrowing, she finds little change in her purchasing habits before and after redundancy. Although she admits that she occasionally used to buy on impulse, it was rare enough. Now, she also has more time to look for bargains and to wait and buy in sales. Neither has she any reluctance to buy in charity shops. As well as buying in them, the family also give things to charity shops. "The kids give their old toys, they recycle them with friends, they swap toys. I hardly ever buy children's clothes. I have a group of friends and we pass on clothes from the older children to the younger ones. I was *always* like that."

Nor does Sheila find that she has to do without things she wants. "We were never very materialistic. I've got a PC and we have two cars, but I regard them as tools for living. I sometimes wonder what people spend their money on. Whenever I'm in a supermarket and I look at all the ready-made meals I think how much nicer and less expensive it is to make them yourself. If you buy take-away pizzas, you could pay £20, £25, and they're not nearly as good as home-made ones. Friday is a treat day here and I bake pizzas from scratch. I make four or five large ones and they cost a fraction of what you would pay otherwise — I use good olives and good cheese, organic flour, yeast out of the freezer." She also has the time now to grow some vegetables and to keep a few hens and ducks. She has an arrangement whereby she trades eggs for organic vegetables with a friend who is in the vegetable business.

Happy as she is with the changes in her life, she also describes some downsides. One is that she has complete responsibility for the housework. While she loves cooking, "cleaning and washing up, washing the clothes, tidying up, washing the floors — I hate it. Housework can be a bit relentless, and the kids can be heavy going."

Several friends are supportive of the recent changes she has made. It's not a huge network, but "certainly enough to show support". Some friends, though, don't understand the choices. Of one in particular, Sheila said, "She wants to know am I doing paid work. She doesn't want to know that I'm editing the school newsletter or organising local neighbourhood events. She wants to know what I'm working at, because that is where the value is, for her."

Her job in RTÉ was not especially glamorous, but "we used to travel around the world quite a lot. People thought I had this amazingly interesting job. But I wasn't interesting because I met interesting people and went to interesting places. An interesting job doesn't make an interesting person. When I spoke to friends who were considering leaving their jobs for similar reasons, one of the main issues that came up was about identity. We are so used to defining other people and ourselves by what job they do. People's eyes glaze over if you say you're a stay-at-home parent. They want to be able to categorise you. You are much easier to define if you are a doctor, a nurse or a teacher."

Sheila has a strong feminist consciousness, which led her to pose the question, "What's the difference between what I'm doing and what my mother did 40 years ago? Because I effectively am in the same situation that my mother was in. She left school at 12. When I was in my late teens, I had complete respect for her, we had a very close relationship — but I would have thought, 'What chance did she have? I'm not going to end up staying at home cooking and looking after children, I'm not going to end up like her.' And I essentially have, and I don't think there's anything particularly wrong by saying that. But she was forced out of school by the economic situation her family was in and then she was forced out of work by social pressure as well as the existence of the marriage bar which meant she couldn't work in a state job after she got married. She really wanted me to finish school and have an education because she hadn't. One of the great advantages of going to university is that it gives you a lot of confidence and you are much less likely to be intimidated by professionals, and that's, I think, what my mother didn't have."

I suggested to Sheila that a major difference between her and her mother was that she had had choices that were not available to her mother. Sheila has contributed financially to her household over the years, and still has the potential to increase her freelance earnings if she wants to. She didn't agree with me: "I didn't have an option, I feel in some ways that I was forced into this," she concluded.

Rose Callan:
From Foreign Exchange to Flexibility and Freedom

Rose Callan was a foreign exchange dealer in an international bank for 14 years. At the end of 1996, in her mid-thirties, she accepted a redundancy package, and these days works part-time as a computer-applications trainer, cares for her two children, and is studying for an Open University degree. Although she earns only a fraction of her previous income, she loves her new way of living for its flexibility and freedom.

"Foreign exchange dealing is quite a stressful job," she says, "so there's always this thing about burnout, and that you're not able to keep it up for a very long time. When I started, I didn't think about the risks, I just did it. Towards the end, though, I wasn't enjoying it. Everything seemed really impossible and with every position you took, you thought it would go wrong, you thought about what might happen, whereas before, you were very optimistic. It was in the back of my mind all the time that I can't keep doing this forever, and I don't want and I don't need this kind of salary. I asked myself why I was working."

Rose recalls a significant discussion she had with her husband, Paul, before giving up her job. A friend died suddenly, and Rose said that if she knew she was going to die, she would change her life. Paul pointed out that she *was* going to die. She realised that she didn't have forever, and she began to think seriously about how she wanted to live. In October 1996, some redundancies were offered at the bank. "I was pregnant at the time, with our first child, and I thought it was a really good opportunity to go."

Haley, her daughter, was born in May 1997, and her son, Thomas, two years later. "I had a very happy pregnancy with them both, because I was so relaxed," she says. "I had the odd stress of getting projects into college or whatever, but it was so much more relaxed than I would have been if I were in a work situation with all that tension." The children both attended a nearby crèche five days a week, until Haley recently started school, and Thomas still goes to the crèche. Rose did not want to care for them full-time, but could not find part-time crèche places. "Unfortunately, the way childcare works is, you have to put them in full-time, to get a place. It's a bit expensive. I work to pay for the childcare really, but I choose it." Rose likes to have the freedom to study and do her training preparation during the day, and to be fresh for the children in the evenings. "I would rather have those days; I feel I need that space for me, so I'm much more patient with them," she explains. "I take them out of the crèche half days here and there, and sometimes full days. And because I'm not under a huge amount of pressure all the time to get them to the crèche, it's more relaxed. They can go in late and we can pick them up early, so it's not quite the same as if we had proper jobs, and how stressful that would be."

"I started in banking straight from school, so I've always worked. That was the hard part, because I always felt that I had to work a nine-to-five. I did miss the bank and found it difficult to motivate myself. I found going from being completely structured to being unstructured *really* difficult. I wasn't getting things done because I didn't have to be anywhere at any particular time." Study and part-time work provided structure for her and the study also taught her to set her own goals and be self-directed, she says, especially since it is delivered through distance learning. Paul, a freelance computer specialist, has always worked in a flexible way, and supports Rose strongly in the changes she has made.

She acknowledges that they are very lucky. "I was earning a lot of money and we bought the house at a good time, so we don't have a huge mortgage. We haven't had to be restricted in terms of groceries. But we have ordinary cars now, and I go to work on a moped. Also, when you have more time, you can actually get things cheaper. You have much more time to sort things out or to go to the sales." She occasionally feels a fleeting envy for "the flash style" some people have. "You think, if you had that diamond hanging out of there. But you have to uncondition yourself really hard about those kind of things; they're just superficial. You also hear of people going away and staying in really fancy places but . . . you see, I've been lucky, in that we had done some of that, and I know that some of those really grand places are unfriendly. And then holidays can be very pressurised as well. People have such a short time and they've got to have a brilliant holiday, so they end up spending an absolute fortune." She would far rather have the opportunities she has now to take long weekends in the west of Ireland, with Paul and the children. She also loves when the four of them take spontaneous days off to go cycling in the Phoenix Park, or to the zoo, both near their home.

Rose's own family background is modest. Her father was the sole earner, her mother emphasised the value of savings, and they also encouraged Rose to do voluntary work. "So I have that grounding there," she says. But she is clear that high earning can create its own lifestyle costs. "The danger is how quickly you get into the other stuff about how you need more. What people think they need when they're in somewhere like the bank, is always something phenomenal, like the bigger cars and flash jewellery and all the signs of doing well. People are just so wound up now about what they need to live. I suppose because they're working so hard they feel they deserve to buy themselves really nice clothes and all this branding stuff. They're working out what their lifestyle cost is now and they're spending a huge amount per month, so if they had to take redundancy, they think they couldn't survive."

She has savings and a pension, which she started when she was in the bank. But she cautions that "you can end up feeling that you have to have too much of that. And then, in a way, that becomes stressful to manage in itself. People in the bank were starting to talk about equities and shares and properties that you had to have if you were going to leave. You'd have to have built up a pension plan of *millions* of pounds. People are just building up these massive nest eggs, and for what? What are they going to do with them?"

Rose thinks it is particularly difficult for people to leave highly specialised jobs like dealing, because they find it hard to imagine doing anything else. "You have to do something completely different. You think you should learn something else, but it's very difficult to do night time study, because you're so wound up." She is also aware of how people can come to feel they "belong" to a company. The message was, "You work for the number one bank in the world; you couldn't possibly work anywhere else. And you're kind of like a god in that business," she laughs. "You're making so much money, not just your salary, but you're making money for the bank, all that sort of stuff, and you're talking about huge amounts of money and about huge responsibility. It's very tough to go voluntarily from that. And yet they're ruthless about staff and about cost cutting and getting rid of people."

She thinks that leaving was a bit easier for her, because she was pregnant when she left. "People say, it's great, she's looking after the kids, that's why she got out of it." Men often feel a certain "ego thing" that makes it more difficult for them to leave, and they often feel a pressure to be the main breadwinner in their families, she observes. "I'll try and teach Thomas that he doesn't have to feel like that," she says.

Rose has time to make a social contribution now, as a member of the local Educate Together school committee. The most precious thing she has is time, she says. "Fund raising for the school, everybody just wants to give you money; they can't give you their time." She also has time to be relaxed with her children, and time for friends, some of whom are people who have cut back on paid work and others who are women who are at home with children all day.

She finds that her social status has declined, compared to when she was in banking. "People used to perk up when I said I was a foreign exchange dealer, and think that I was really interesting. And now when I say I'm a trainer, I can see people shutting off and that's really disconcerting. You think, God, I was obviously just interesting because of my job. And it's also terrible, the labels you get, being at home. You see immediately — people's faces — and they don't mean it, but they just think, she mustn't be very interesting. But I probably know more about politics and what's going on because I listen to the radio and I've time to read a newspaper and stuff. If they knew how interesting I was when I was a foreign exchange dealer, when I was totally focused on statistics coming out of the States," she laughs. "In that kind of job, you have to listen to loads of conversations about prices and things like that. Even when you're out — I found myself sometimes talking to one person and listening to other conversations. So I'm much more aware of those kinds of things. I'm probably a much nicer person."

In the longer term, Rose is not sure what she will do. She would like something a bit more challenging than computer applications training and she may open a business of her own. But she definitely does not want to work full-time, and would love to see more companies offering part-time work. She realises that, given the way most companies are structured, it has its disadvantages, however, especially when one enjoys a challenge. "You'd have to be realistic and say that if you are going to do a three-day week, you are going to have to swallow your pride in terms of appearing to be successful, or doing well. That was one thing I found when I went into the training work. I found that I wanted to get involved in other projects they were doing in the company, something really challenging and interesting, and I always had to bite my tongue and say to myself that I have chosen to do a three-day week, I can't start getting involved in something, because I won't be there for meetings." Nevertheless, she loves the freedom of her current lifestyle so much that these seem like small sacrifices. "I've got much more flexibility and I'm very happy at the moment. It's really brilliant," she says.

Common Experiences

The downshifters all reached some kind of turning point, where they decided they had had enough of their frenzied lives and jobs, and that it was time for change. While Ida, Henry, Sheila and Rose have been lucky because they received retirement or redundancy lump sums, they were able to make efficient use of the money they received, because they had always been accustomed to living within their means. They tend to pay cash for purchases, and to save until they can afford them, continuing to avoid debt. Having reduced the pressures from the world of paid work, many of them comment on their improved health. They have time to cook healthily also, often using organic ingredients. Although organic ingredients are often more expensive than non-organic, and cooking from scratch can be time-consuming, the whole process works out a lot cheaper than buying the convenience foods that so many people rely on. They are able to contribute to their communities and children's education, and feel more connected to their local environment.

Nor have they given up wider ambitions. Rose is doing a degree and may open a business. Ida is also studying and plans to do some freelance journalism when she finishes her degree. Sheila and her partner plan to travel extensively when their children are older. Henry is always learning and developing his knowledge as a healer.

They have worked out the things that they want to prioritise, and some of them have thereby had to make some compromises. Eoghan misses the creative buzz of working with other people. Sheila, Rose and Ida have all experienced a loss of status in turning their backs on the full-time labour market. Undoubtedly, there are gender differences in the experiences of downshifters. Women who cut back on careers may be accused of sabotaging the independence of women in general. This is an outmoded view, given the advances in feminist thinking in recent years, and the recognition that both women and men benefit from doing a mixture of paid and unpaid work, without overdoing either. In spite of the downsides, however, a strong theme in the stories is the freedom and empowerment they experience, as a result of taking responsibility for the shape of their lives.

Chapter Eight

IT'S NOT JUST A FAD: STARTING EARLY TO THINK OUTSIDE THE BOX

A common reaction to stories of downshifting is that the people involved are simply reacting to the stressed lifestyles of boom periods. As this chapter shows, however, not all those seeking to live balanced lives are fleeing from high-flying pressurised jobs, or from the economic boom that hit Ireland in the 1990s. Several chose their lifestyles long before we had ever heard the expression "Celtic Tiger". They are fortunate enough to have known from early in their adulthood what they wanted or, just as importantly, didn't want. I refer to them as long-timers, who show that living a balanced life is not some kind of short-lived fad.

Trish Hehir and Mícheál Ó Raghallaigh: Music in Meath

Trish Hehir (34) and Mícheál Ó Raghallaigh (31) live in rural Meath, with their children Muireann (10), Maebh (6), Tadhg (4) and Laoise (2). Both Trish and Mícheál combine a variety of self-employed work with bringing up their children together. Trish's work is mostly in adult education — personal development courses, evaluation work and community arts — along with some music teaching. She also does a variety of voluntary work in the local community. Mícheál is a well-known traditional musician who plays in a variety of bands and settings. He also repairs musical instruments and does some music teaching. Neither of them has ever considered full-time employment in a nine-to-five situation as an attractive option, although Trish held a full-time contract post in adult education for two-and-a-half years and Mícheál worked in a music shop in Dublin for a short time. Their combined pre-tax income in 2000–01 was in the region of £20,000 (€25,400).

Mícheál grew up on his parents' farm, just across the road from their home. The farm was small (34 acres) and Mícheál explains that he and his brothers and sisters grew up understanding that they could not always have everything they wanted. There was comfort, but little extravagance, although music and musical instruments were always available and considered extremely important, and the couple have continued to emphasise music with their own family. This upbringing helped him decide from early on what his priorities are. "I know people who are different," he says. "One couple both work at full time jobs and they've got this massive house and they go on foreign holidays and they say they have no money, yet they spent ten grand on doing up their kitchen." "That would have built half of what we did in this house," adds Trish. "You know, some people's idea of 'no money' is hilarious."

They bought their house in 1993. "Muireann was a few months old and we had nowhere to stay," says Mícheál. "We had to have something. If it had been fifty miles from my parents, we mightn't have done it." His mother encouraged them to first rent and then buy the house, and his parents' continued support for their way of life is very important to both of them.

They say that they were lucky to buy when they did, "That's the biggest thing. I mean, the house was £22,500 (€28,575), on an acre," says Mícheál. It was built in 1910, and it was "a wreck" when they moved in. They lived in fairly basic conditions at first, "with a microwave and one gas ring". They have slowly done it up and extended it over the years and it is now a beautiful, bright and comfortable family home.

They borrowed from the county council to buy the house, and later borrowed from the local credit union, to finance home improvements. They found difficulty with banks, when they sought home improvement loans. "The bank wouldn't give us those kind of loans because we didn't have permanent jobs," says Trish. "I was laughed out of several banks because I had no permanent job. I mean, they'd give me money for a car or a holiday, and I'd say I don't want those, I'd prefer a house."

They have learned not to worry too much about money, having discovered that a cheque usually arrives from one of their "jobs", when they need to pay for something. "You are thinking, how are we going to pay the oil bill, and the next thing something arrives in the post — maybe even four or five of them," explains Trish. They don't buy much apart from essentials, and they manage well. "We don't have an extravagant lifestyle," says Trish. "I don't buy clothes — I love looking, but I rarely buy." Mícheál and Trish's father made their kitchen cupboards for a fraction of the price it would take to buy them. They rarely go out. Neither of them enjoys the pub scene, although Mícheál plays in pubs. "I usually end up with a pint glass of water," he says.

Trish likes to cook fresh wholesome food and she has the time to cook from scratch instead of buying ready-made or convenience foods, which in itself means savings on grocery bills. They also try to grow some of their own vegetables in the garden. They buy other essentials as cheaply as possible, often through *Buy and Sell* magazine. The family runs one car, which they bought from savings. They reckon that if one of them worked full-time, they would need a second car for driving the children to the school bus and to other activities. They don't have holidays as such, although they recently bought an old caravan for £500 (€635), which needs a lot of cleaning up, but will allow the family to travel with Mícheál in the summer, when he conducts music workshops at venues all over Ireland.

Mícheál makes money "in theory" from playing. He is involved in one purely commercial venture with a band, and they have produced a CD and have a second one ready. They are not connected with a record company and are doing the distribution themselves. But the important thing for him is that they have control of what they play. He also had a solo CD venture launched recently, which adds to the family's annual income. He is certain that he will not take a "job" in the future, because it is important to him to have the freedom to be able to decide what he does. "I don't know about full-time work in the future," says Trish. "I can see myself doing something more consistent, maybe, but not 'til I'm in my forties."

Family is their current priority and other work is organised to facilitate that. "They're only small for a short time," says Trish. Both are also adamant that, although they are doing exactly what they want to do, and are very happy doing it, their way of living is far from simple: "The question is juggling the time — you don't always have it," says Mícheál. "Four children don't allow that, you can't work repairing instruments, if they need you." "I couldn't work a nine-to-five with the kids," says Trish. "I would never see them and I'd be narky all the time. We wouldn't have had four kids in the first place if we'd had a lifestyle other than this. We were here one afternoon — we had the dinner at three o'clock, then we were playing a board game afterwards — and we were just saying, it's great to do this with the kids, in the middle of the day, in the middle of the week. It doesn't happen all the time, there are lots of days you're busy trying to get something done or one of us is out, but it's important that somebody is around for them."

The children are allowed to watch some television, and they see the toys and games that are available, as well as seeing what other children have. They get lots of gifts from aunts and uncles and grandparents, and of course from parents at birthdays and Christmas. But the children are not demanding, and both Trish and Mícheál are clear that they say "no" to them without feeling guilty. "One reason we feel the children are not so demanding is, because we're around, we're not afraid to say 'no' to them. We've said no to them about things since they were small. I think if we weren't around as much, we'd be very inclined to give into them more easily. Definitely, that's a factor in not being afraid to say no," says Trish.

They are aware of some downsides of their choices, although these are minor in comparison to the benefits. One downside of not having a great deal of discretionary income is that they are not always able to join in activities with friends or take expensive hotel breaks, at a cost that would cover "three weeks' groceries" for the family.

It can also be hard to explain to other people what they actually do for a living. "People want a slot they can put you in," says Mícheál. "Teacher is the easiest one for people to understand, because they presume you teach in a school and that you work from nine to five." "Even my friends still don't know really what I do," adds Trish. They don't know other people who have made the choices they have made, and since they don't consider that they are doing anything special, they don't consider themselves part of a social trend. The way they live demands so much planning, says Mícheál, that "I'd be surprised if people at this crack know each other, because they wouldn't have time."

Trish's tips: "It is complicated, you have to lower your standards, but that's not the right word at all. You have to kind of cut your cloth — you know? You can't expect to be able to have an expensive lifestyle, if you are going to make choices to cut back on the amount of work you do. And we are happy with that, others wouldn't be. You have to change your way of thinking; you can't expect the same level of things and of material possessions as people on larger incomes. You have to decide what you want, what you really need — you don't need all the trappings."

Mícheál's tips: "You really have to have the right person involved with you, if you're in a relationship. Otherwise, you may forget it. If Trish began to want furs at this point in our lives, I would resent *her wanting them, and she would resent me for not wanting her to have them. So you have to think alike. There's no hard and fast rules, though. And you can't say what you advise somebody else to do, because it's a case of horses for courses."*

Richard Douthwaite: Richness through Simple Living

Richard Douthwaite is a leading world thinker on alternative or "new" economics. He makes a living as a freelance journalist and writer. His best-known books are *The Growth Illusion* and *Short Circuit*. He was born in England, and came with his wife, Mary, and their three children to Westport in 1974. Richard and his family have always lived simply on a small income, but he considers himself rich in many ways.

Mary and Richard met while still in their teens. They were married with one child when he went to university, aged 25. "I was a journalist and then I realised that I didn't have the background to the stories that I was dealing with, so I went to university. The choice of university was based on where we could live on our boat — a fishing boat that we bought in Holland and converted. So I went to Essex University. I thought I was going to be doing politics, but we did a combined first year — politics, sociology and economics and I saw immediately that the real power lay with economics."

After his degree, he got a chance to do postgraduate study in economics, in Jamaica, on a British government *Study and Serve* scheme. Tuition fees and a stipend were paid, on condition that one worked for a Commonwealth government for a time after qualifying. "We all went to Jamaica, and we had two small children when we arrived there. We had very little money — the stipend that I got was not for married people at all — the assumption was that you were single. But we had some money from the sale of our boat and this enabled us to buy some land in the hills above Kingston — I was at university in Kingston — so we built a tiny house there — although it was the biggest that the local builder had ever built. He was normally used to building ten-by-tens, and ours was twenty by twenty. Mary got a job teaching at a school in the mornings and I attended university three afternoons for my course. Essentially I was interested in development economics and thought that the perspective you would get from studying it in a developing country would be far different than if you had gone to a British university, for example. So then I worked for a year in the central planning unit of the Jamaican government, on a study on the effects of tourism on the Jamaican economy."

After this, Richard set up and managed a boat yard in Jamaica for the Jamaica Co-operative Union, the umbrella body for the island's fishing co-ops. When he handed that over to a local worker, he was offered a two-year contract as a government economic advisor in Montserrat. By this time, the couple's two sons, Ború and Joss, were seven and nine. Their daughter Lucy was born in Montserrat. When the contract was up, they decided to move to Ireland. "We could have stayed in Montserrat for another two years, but we wanted to give the children a permanent base. Mary, whose father was Irish, and I hadn't lived anywhere in particular as children, we had moved around, and we wanted our children to feel they belonged — it's important for identity. At that time, the first OPEC oil crisis had struck, and we realised that western economic systems were very vulnerable. We had been reading John Seymour's books and we wanted to buy land and try to be self-reliant.

"We arrived in Ireland in 1974, and eventually settled on Westport as a place to live. We spent all the money we had from the sale of our home in Montserrat on 30 acres of hillside. We subsequently had to sell three sites, in order to finance cutting a roadway, and providing electricity to the site buyers. The money from the third site went towards our own house. Mary did the block-laying and I did the heavy lifting. We bought a tractor, to turn a cement-mixer on the back and carry stuff up the hill. We are still building — money and time rarely have coincided — either you're very busy and you have money, or you have time to build, but no money. And things get to a point where you're reasonably comfortable, and other things become more pressing."

They didn't retain the ideal of being a self-sufficient nuclear family doing everything for themselves. But they continue to grow some of their own food and fuel. In the early days, they also ran a business based on Mary's work as an occupational therapist. With 13 employees, they made leather kits for occupational therapy, using scrap leather from shoe factories all over Ireland. But they did not enjoy the experience and ran into financial difficulties, fearing for a time that the bank would claim their house.

"After that, I went back into journalism, writing about environmental and economic issues — largely to do with the west of Ireland because that was where I had a competitive advantage over Dublin-based people — gold mining and salmon farming, for example. I became heavily involved with the Irish Green Party, and helped develop an early version of their economic policies. That led to a major change for me. All the time I'd been at university I'd been worried about economic growth and how infinite economic growth was going to be compatible with a finite planet. I had been convinced by some of the arguments in the book *The Limits to Growth*, when that came out in 1972, and in particular that the problem wasn't going to be resource constraints in terms of mercury, or rock phosphates or energy, but it was going to be pollution and pressure on sinks. And so, towards the end of the 1980s when information began to come in about global warming and the reality of it, I thought, we've reached the limits to growth, in fact, we've exceeded them and we're not going to be able to run the economy in the same way. Either we have to find a different form of growth or we have to find a way of changing the economic system so it doesn't need growth, somebody is going to be writing a book about this. I looked for one and nobody did, and so I thought, right, I'll do it myself." That book was *The Growth Illusion*.

"I spent three years writing *The Growth Illusion*. I had no funding, because I had no track record, although I had a gentleman's agreement with The Lilliput Press that they would publish it. I juggled it with articles. I'd finish a chapter, then go back to journalism. I found I couldn't do the two simultaneously. One involved the thinking process and the development of ideas and the other was very much more of an adrenaline rush for an immediate deadline. Mary played a very important role in that book. She was essentially the reader that I was writing for. She would read through a chapter — normally she would read it in bed at night — and if she fell asleep over it, then it was too boring."

They have never had much money. "I was making some income from journalism while writing *The Growth Illusion*, but it was very difficult — freelance journalism is a very bad way of selling information. Had Mary not continued to work, it would have been quite impossible. But we were very hard up during that period. We couldn't run a vehicle and we depended on neighbours — anything heavy that arrived had to be pushed up the hill in a wheelbarrow, this sort to thing. But in fact it was liberating to know that we could manage on very little. I thought that *The Growth Illusion* would open doors and sell very well, but it didn't. It sold very well for a book of its sort, but it would have needed to sell ten times as many to repay the effort that went into writing it. But it enabled me to get financial support for *Short Circuit*, to go round the world doing research. That's why I say I feel very privileged.

"Nevertheless, to a great extent, what I have been able to do has been as a result of Mary's sacrifice and it's only now that the income pressures are receding and she is able to get the time to do the things that she wants to do that she's been itching to do for years — I mean she wants to paint and she's never felt that she has been able to justify taking the time to do it. Essentially, she has given me the freedom to follow my road and it's only belatedly that I can now let her have the freedom. Even so, it's not a clear road for her because there are still family commitments. Her mother lived for 18 months at the back of our house in a granny flat, until she died early in 2002. We have another little house that we converted from a workshop when our second son took a job as an occupational therapist with the Western Health Board in Westport. He was living there with his wife and two small children until two years ago. And that also interfered with her freedom because there were little ones around and she loved playing the role of grandmother."

When their own three children were small, they did not demand things the family couldn't afford. "Maybe it would have been healthy if there had been a reaction against how we were living," says Richard. "We got TV only quite late and had no electricity for a long time. The ESB had wanted more money than we had to bring it up to our hill." He feels it may have been a little hard on his daughter Lucy sometimes at one school she attended. "Most of the kids came from extremely wealthy families and so they would come in posh cars and we'd come in a van. When our second son, Joss, left home for the first time — he was going to teach as a volunteer in Zimbabwe — he thanked us for making his life so hard that nothing would seem tough in future."

Now that the children are adults, they share their parents' interests and "live the same kind of lifestyle to a gratifying extent". They have travelled and been involved in projects such as permaculture, agricultural engineering and other environmental work. Both Joss and Lucy, with their respective partners, are working abroad, in order to save money to build houses on sites that Richard and Mary have given them, and Ború, their oldest son, is also building on the sea, near Westport. Richard is looking forward to having them close by again. "We have a sort of *clachan* [a cluster of houses] already. There's the big house and then the small house, and the granny flat as well as workshops and sheds and we carry on building."

Richard attributes the close family relationships to Mary's efforts. "Mary is the person who keeps the family together and I think there were never problems with the children and now our relationships are very close and we work on projects together. I editedBorú's book on how technology develops. When Lucy had essays to do as part of her nursing, there was always a crisis, and she would come home and the whole family would help with her essays. We'd have them done in two hours."

Richard and Mary still live on a very small income, although it is slightly more secure than it was in the past. Their current joint taxable income is between £10,000 [€12,700] and £12,000 [€15,240]. "Within the last two or three years, we have moved out of the position of worrying about when the next cheques will come — that's the stressful thing — you know, wondering is it going to come this week or not. Having an extra £2,000 is a cushion. We have absolutely no savings, we have no pension provisions, but we have no debts either." Neither would they be keen to see their children take out mortgages.

Richard's parents have also helped them a great deal. "My family has always been there to support us. My father and mother are still alive and they helped us when we needed to get out of the trouble with the bank [after the business folded]. If we ever did run into a crisis, they would be there again. Joss was shot when he was in Zimbabwe and again my father played a big role. We didn't have to pay for his treatment, but nevertheless, there was this huge support through the crisis.

"But I think I have always been extremely confident — I've never really been worried that things won't work out all right for me. First of all, I've never really been interested in money, I've never been motivated by money at all. I feel I'm extremely privileged, because I can do the things that really interest me, that really excite me. I don't have to put up with doing things just to earn the money." For example, he does unpaid work in the field of New Economics, which is his passion. He is especially active in Feasta, the Foundation for the Economics of Sustainability.

He works very hard, although he is conscious of the need to balance intellectual and physical work. He normally starts work about five in the morning, and writes, e-mails and does other deskwork until one. After lunch, he does some physical work. "It's a very efficient way of working, because if you're digging or cutting wood, or something like that, it frees your mind for thinking about the things you've been working on — you see perspectives you wouldn't have." They usually have an evening meal at about 6.00 p.m., then he reads for a while and retires at about 9.30. They find Westport a good place to live, as many people in the area want an alternative lifestyle. Mary and Richard's children and grandchildren are likely to be present in their lives in the future, so they will have the support of an extended family as they get older. However, by running a business in the early days, and through Mary's work for the Western Care Association, they have also got to know a lot of people in the mainstream community. "So we have the best of both worlds," he says.

Mari-aymone Djeribi and Dominic Stevens: Appreciating Slowness

Mari-aymone Djeribi and Dominic Stevens live in Leitrim. They work mostly from home, Dominic as an architect, and Mari-aymone as a publisher and graphic designer. Both in their early thirties and with two children, Ezekiel (2½) and Nour (four months), they did not always plan to live in a rural area. But they have always been concerned with quality of life and doing work that they enjoy. Entering a new phase of their lives, having a family and wanting to build a place of their own, they would have had to work extremely hard to make enough money to stay in Dublin, where they previously rented a flat in the city centre. They found that they could afford to buy a site in Leitrim. Because their work still takes them to Dublin sometimes, they chose to build close to a railway station, to avoid driving. Currently, they each do their paid work every morning while a neighbour comes in to mind the children. They take turns caring for them in the afternoons. They have a small mortgage and no other debts. Mari-aymone considers herself good with money, in the sense that "I don't panic when I have none".

They both love their work and they feel that the less money they need to make from it, the better they can do it. Publishing and architecture, they say, are things that can be done on a commercial basis and that can make a lot of money, but the downside of this may be that the quality of the work suffers. Living relatively cheaply, as they do, gives them the freedom to work slowly, at a high standard, and to take on the kinds of work they want, turning down what they don't want. "Basically, we choose," explains Mari-aymone. "I've been doing this for a while, I've chosen who I work for and what I do, and I choose not to do some work. That's always been very important for me."

She considers publishing to be her main work, but she makes her money mostly from graphic design. "I moved to Leitrim and I'm not on the Internet by choice and I thought I'd have to convince clients that I was still available and all that, but in fact, it's been the complete opposite. I thought I wouldn't have to make the effort to get less work, but I think I will have to."

Dominic has chosen to keep his architectural practice at a size where he can be personally involved with all of his projects. He employs one other architect, but has no intention of expanding his business "If my clients allow the fact that it takes a bit longer, then I'm happy," he explains.

They both believe that the kind of creative work they do benefits from spending time away from the current project. "In my work, I appreciate slowness," Dominic explains. "A lot of the times you're creative — it's when you're doing the dishes. The time you're looking after your child is a really lovely time, but it's also a time you're peripherally thinking about things. To build that slowness into your life is lovely. And sitting on trains is another thing. I have four hours a week when, on the way into town, I work and I design things and on the way back I read something. It's a great time. This house — this land that we have to look after — is also one of those tools that slow us down. And slowing down liberates you, really."

Another reason for not wanting to take on too much paid work is that they are committed to sharing childcare, and being fully involved with Ezekiel and Nour. Mari-aymone explains, "Dominic is a very 'present' father — he wants to be — my dad was never there. And it is very important that we are both there. It is also something that would have been more difficult in town because of peer pressure, I think. If we hadn't moved out, we would have to explain on a daily basis that we weren't trying to make much money — so we are actually getting a break."

Their timber and straw-bale house, which is highly insulated and easy to heat, was also built slowly. They built it themselves, assisted by two students of architecture and several friends. At first, they camped on the site at weekends, and as move-in time approached, were there constantly. When I visited them in February 2001, there was still a lot of cosmetic work to do, but they were very happy with the comfort and warmth they had had over the winter. "Coming up to the move, we were slightly nervous but there was no problem at all," says Mari-aymone. "I think the slow occupancy of the area is great, the fact that we camped, and went to and from Dublin. And because I'm a city person, I always thought, if I end up in the country, I'll be worried about what is outside there at night. And because we actually lived and camped outside there, I know what's outside. We kind of moved inwards to this space that we made. That was really, really important. Our soul was here before we moved in."

"The night we first came and slept here," adds Dominic, "we walked down from the fields up there, into a house that we'd been making, as opposed to driving up the road and putting our key in the door. So it was a very different way of occupying the place that you live. As an architect that's something I'm interested in also. A house is kind of a hard-won, important thing, and it's good to take it all slowly and appreciate it."

The process of building their house helped them to get to know local suppliers and trades people. The couple have learned from their neighbours and they appreciate the ways that many rural people are not locked into a job for life, but can turn their hand to whatever needs doing, be it fixing a roof, fixing a car, growing things, or looking after animals. They have also got to know people through buying locally produced goods such as organic meat and vegetables, and through using their public library.

They are both very reflective people and have thought carefully about the sort of life they want to lead. They are also lucky that their work can be carried out wherever they are. Nevertheless, they think that what they have done is quite ordinary, that they are not exceptional and that creative options are open to everybody. "I would view the kind of decisions that we're making as pragmatic and not some airy-fairy dream," says Dominic. "Most of these decisions to do with houses and cars, and childcare, they're the biggest decisions you make, and most people don't make them, they just do 'what you do'. You could certainly assume huge debt, be it a mortgage or whatever, and your life becomes extremely complicated and isn't fun anymore. There's this kind of accepted thing that, well, okay, things get serious now. So we feel like we've been able to slide out of that. I think there's many more people like us who can do it, especially since, in Ireland, rural depopulation is a problem. It's not that you have a duty to, but it kind of just makes sense."

"We didn't set up going on a mission," adds Mari-aymone. "We really — maybe even selfishly — designed our life to suit us. And it turns out that it actually is a more caring life. We're extremely concerned with the environment, but we didn't forget about us. It's not like a retreat — it's very much our life and we've really pushed towards comfort, but it's more kind of felt comfort and chosen comfort. So it wasn't this paring down — you know, when you think of downshifting you always think of people who had Mercs and big houses and good living and then rough it. We're not roughing it at all, we're more comfortable here than in our flat in Merrion Square. And what we don't have is things that it turns out we don't need — or we don't need as intensively as we had access to."

Dominic adds that while they have had some puzzled reactions from other people, most people have been interested and supportive. Those friends who helped with building the house have a stake in it. Some friends they see less often than when they were in Dublin, but the upside of that is that when people do visit, there is time to relax together. "They come and visit, we eat with them and we sit around with them and it's so much better than seeing them five times a week in a coffee shop with music blasting in the background. So we haven't lost out," says Mari-aymone.

She continues, "I think we're very lucky with our jobs — the kinds of things we're interested in, but — I hope it doesn't sound moralising or anything — I don't think that a lot of people realise that being happy is the most important thing and it's not so difficult. You know, there's a lot of stuff that you can let go that is not that difficult. But I think it's always been my guiding principle that happy is the only thing I could do, to make my life worthwhile. And in fact, when you do that, it's not a selfish thing, because you can't be happy if people around you are not happy."

They are very pleased with how things have worked out so far, even though it has been a lot of hard work. "At the start, we certainly had no idea of what it entailed and how much work it was. I wouldn't do it again, but I wouldn't have done it in any other way. It requires a lot of imagination," says Mari-aymone. "It takes a lot of creative energy to think, okay, what can I have if I can have everything?" When their children are grown, they do not rule out a move back to a city, but for the foreseeable future, Leitrim is home.

Mari-aymone's tips: *"What's important is not to do something too drastic. I think a lot of people think, Yeah, I don't like my life, let's dump my job. And I think it doesn't work that way, because if you dump all the stuff that is your life, you end up losing yourself as well. Change very, very gradually. I think it's good to actually do some thinking before you lose the job you wanted to let go. It's very important that you make the decision as well, before you have to be reactive. But I think a big change and a happy change can't come out of a huge jump."*

Dominic's tips: *"Something I say to clients when they commission me to design something — the first thing they have to do is to think about what they want. And when they are thinking about what they want, it shouldn't be connected with what they think things cost, because there's always choice around these things. I think people often feel constrained by what things cost, as much as what other people do. You know, you do what other people do and you also do what you think you can afford. And they're both the wrong places to start."*

Laragh Neelin:
Living Lightly

Laragh Neelin is 59 and has always done things differently. Born in Canada of an Irish mother and Irish-Canadian father, she lives in Dublin and in Ottawa, Canada. Renting rooms in homes she owns in both Dublin and Ottawa covers her own accommodation expenses and commuting travel. She also has a cushion of savings. When people ask her what she does for a living, she doesn't always find it easy to give a simple description. "For one thing, if I say I'm retired, most people don't think I'm as old as I am. And sometimes I say 'as little as possible', and sort of make a joke out of it. Some people say, oh, you should say you're in real estate, but I figure that sounds too grand. So I usually say — you know, if I'm being totally honest — I say 'I rent rooms in my home'."

Laragh rents two rooms in her Dublin city centre mews home to students or visiting contract workers, on a short-term basis. She also rents three rooms in her home in Ottawa, again mostly to students, sometimes paying a local man to supervise arrivals and departures, and keeping a room for herself to use. She prefers to rent like this, because if the relationship does not work out, it's easier to ask someone to leave, or it's not too long to wait to the end of the rental period. She is also adamant that she does not want to rent long-term to people who rent because they cannot afford to own their own home. "I wouldn't want to be a landlord. I feel people should own their own home and I wouldn't want to make money that way," she explains. Instead, she provides a service to people temporarily in need of accommodation. She spends a good deal of time arranging the various lets. "I use the Internet a lot. I couldn't do the renting in Canada without it. And I use a free website in Dublin, which keeps costs down. Internet use also reduced my phone calls and I don't need to buy newspapers or magazines."

Laragh lives frugally but well and considers that her lifestyle is sustainable, a reasonable example of "low impact", or "living lightly" on the earth. She has attended a couple of permaculture courses and reads a lot about Feng Shui. She is active in the Dublin Food Co-op, and is very careful about all her purchasing habits, both in terms of costs, packaging and environmental damage. "I've still got some Ecover cleanser and toilet cleaner I bought in bulk, five years ago. I supply all the stuff here in the house, because I don't like chemical smells in my home. And all the paint is natural. I don't use chipboard in any of my houses. I compost and try to recycle and reuse sustainable products everywhere. I'm even starting to find some organic clothing now." She actually buys very few clothes, as she considers that she already has enough quality clothing and she alters what she has to suit changing fashions. She inherited several tweed suits, dresses and a grey squirrel coat from her mother. She has even reused some items of her father and her uncle. When she does buy, she looks for bargains in sales (at least 50 per cent off) and at second-hand charity shops. She keeps fit and healthy by walking, t'ai chi, eating organic, doing a bi-annual internal herbal cleanse, and using only herbal medicines. She has very few medical bills, although she does have dental costs.

Laragh gave up the car for environmental and economic reasons nine years ago. She walks everywhere in the city, uses public transport as much as possible for travel further afield, the occasional taxi, and hires a car when she needs one. "I can't wait to get my bus pass in three years at 62," she laughs. Although it is a huge saving not having to run a car, she is currently reconsidering. "The hardest thing about giving up the car in Ireland was refusing a lift late at night with somebody who had been drinking, or taking lifts with drivers of unknown ability. And even public transport isn't all that safe, all the time. So I'm rethinking the car thing, certainly."

Although she travels quite a bit, she tries to keep air travel to a minimum for environmental reasons and nearly always stays with relations or friends. She has a wide network of friends she can stay with, in Ireland, Britain, and Canada, and has cousins in Florida for a winter vacation. "The idea of going off on an expensive holiday is out, really. I pay my airfare and I think that's a lot. You know, I was trying to remember the last time I had been in a hotel. But the thing about renting rooms here short term is that occasionally I have an empty room and friends can stay with me too."

A chequered past has brought Laragh to her current position. She has never passed up an opportunity for change or self-improvement. She believes one should live for today, not yesterday or tomorrow. She trained as a journalist and, among other things, worked as a contract piping-design draftsman, owned and operated a whole-food store, and cared for her elderly parents and an uncle. She remembers her parents' experience of the Depression of the 1930s in Canada, and suspects that these second-hand memories have helped her live frugally and sustainably most of her life.

Laragh considers herself "pretty normal" but she started learning lessons about how to live lightly early in life. Early on, while unemployed for a while in Montreal in the 1960s, she realised that she could save money by cooking from scratch and that the fact that she didn't have to buy work clothes also saved her money. When she moved to Texas, she bought a car, as everybody did there, and learned how to do auto maintenance, in order to keep her bills down. While in Texas she had the opportunity to learn piping design on the job at full pay.

Her work also took her all over Eastern Canada. In one town, rather than pay expensive motel bills, she lived in her jeep with her two dogs for six weeks, and became aware of more possibilities for living cheaply. Later, she bought a 26-foot motor home, where she lived for a few years travelling to different job sites around Ontario province. Since the motor home was self-contained, she never paid for parking, using public parks and the occasional night-watchman job in exchange for parking and electricity. In 1982 she bought a small house in the countryside, just outside Ottawa, which she still owns. She used tax-free savings and a small government grant to finance 85 per cent of the purchase. The vendor agreed to hold a small mortgage, as Laragh did not want to borrow from a bank, and Laragh had a $50–a-month mortgage for three years, after which time she owned the house free and clear.

In 1985, Laragh's ageing parents sold their house. Her mother moved into a nursing home, and Laragh and her father moved into a house bought on the proceeds from the sale of her parents' home. When he died, her mother wasn't happy in the nursing home, so she and Laragh sold the house and bought a more suitable apartment on one level. By this time, Laragh had learned a lot about buying and selling houses, so she got a very good deal on the house and was able to invest some leftover money. In Canada, the government pays the elderly a state pension plus a guaranteed income supplement, so Laragh's mother also had that allowance. When her father died, they also discovered that he had owned a share in a valuable small family farm, which Laragh also managed to sell at a good price. Using some of the proceeds from that sale, Laragh took her mother home to Ireland for a visit.

Even though her mother was quite frail, and using a walker, the visit was a success, and they arranged to return for Laragh's uncle's eightieth birthday the following year. He lived on an acre in South County Dublin, and invited them to stay on with him, as the people who had been caring for him were no longer able to do so. The garden was overgrown, but Laragh was able to restore the fruit trees and the vegetable garden. Her uncle had been paying a housekeeper, so now he paid Laragh in kind, providing accommodation and expenses. They were all able to live cheaply and well.

Her mother needed a lot of care in the few years before she died, but some money was available from her old age pension and from Canadian real estate profits to buy expensive equipment. The bed alone cost £12,000, but it allowed Laragh to do most of the nursing care herself. She only employed occasional sitters to stay with the elderly pair when she wanted to go out, and she used a mobile phone, in the days when they were rare, to keep in touch.

Three years after the move to Ireland, Laragh's mother died at 85. By this time, her uncle was beginning to have age-related problems — he would wander out of his garden and get disoriented. In 1993, they decided to move to the city centre, where there would be a variety of places to go on foot or by public transport together. They sold the house and rented at first, eventually finding the mews house where Laragh now lives. The layout and its small courtyard were ideal for her uncle. When Laragh wanted to go somewhere, she often would take him with her. As with her mother, they used the mobile phone and a room monitor, so that he could be left at home alone and they did not have to be together constantly.

When her uncle had a stroke at age 85, Laragh was told that he hadn't long to live, and decided, against medical advice, to take him home from hospital and nurse him herself.

With foresight, she had negotiated a deal with the medical supply company that they would take back the expensive bed used for her mother, but that they would sell it again to her at the same second-hand price if she needed it for her uncle. He lived for another year and a half. During this time, they visited Venezuela, where some of his books were being published, and Canada — all using her mother's Canadian wheelchair.

Laragh made very conscious choices regarding the elderly people in her life, in order to maintain quality of life for them. "The medical system is self-perpetuating, it's about job creation, and they try to pressure you into supervised care. I don't think there's usually any need for it. In Canada they tried to say my Dad had Alzheimer's, but then I discovered that in the day-care system there, the hospital got more money for Alzheimer's patients than for other elderly." She also questions the ties of the medical establishment to drug companies. "Over here, they tried to say my uncle had Alzheimer's — and I think with 95 per cent of the patients, it is mini-strokes and not Alzheimer's at all." The Irish doctor wanted to treat him with a new Alzheimer's drug, as part of a drug-company research project. "I realised that it's drug-company money over here, rather than government money, that may influence Alzheimer's diagnoses. So we didn't accept that."

Laragh recognises that she had what she calls a "good start in life". She was an only child and had a good education. She also inherited property, which she maximised so that it now brings her a small income. While caring for her parents in their old age, she says, "I took care of money, I made money out of their money." In most of the property deals that followed her parents' sale of their house, there was money left over to provide a cushion of savings. She also considers that she is lucky with money and negotiations for property sales to speculators.

The rent from her various lettings "allows me to live in a house I can't afford. I couldn't afford to run this house and leave that much money tied up, without lodgers. And the same in Ottawa." For the future, she intends to sell at least one house and maximise the income from both her Canadian and Dublin properties. She also loves hill walking and is considering buying a small place in Killarney, where she could live for the winter, renting it out in the summer. "The idea about Killarney is that you can just get on the train and be in Dublin in four hours. I'd keep a small place here in Dublin, that I would rent to one or two students in the winter, and live here in the summer as well as in Canada." Currently, she is trying to simplify her life radically, by rationalising her possessions further, and getting her papers down to "shoebox size", which would make travelling and living in different places even easier.

ം ം ം

Barry Jones:
Looking Beyond Common Sense

In 1987, when he was in his mid-thirties, Barry Jones gave up what many would consider the perfect job, as a permanent, pensionable lecturer in Italian at University College Dublin. After that, he lived on his boat for a time and earned a modest income chartering around the Irish coast every summer. He and his wife, Finola O'Carroll, an archaeologist, bought a small cottage in rural Meath; Barry continued his charter work until early 2000, when he gave it up in order to be a full-time parent to their two children, Beannán (12) and Lucy (5).

Barry is very critical of contemporary society. Until he was about 26, he had a series of jobs. He started in the Royal Air Force and also worked as a psychiatric nurse, and as a civil servant, among other things. Although he disliked the Air Force, he says that "all their ideologies are more honest, in a way, the pomp and the uniform". He believes that most ideology is passed over as "common sense" or taken-for-granted ways of thinking and doing things. When he started academic life, as a mature student at the age of 26, he developed radical interests and excelled in philosophy and critical theory.

These interests were the reason he got his UCD lecturing job in the first place, but after a while, the department seemed to be taking a direction he disliked. "The language departments became very much service departments to commerce and economics, with the emphasis on language, which is missing the point really. I was never comfortable teaching language, because that's performance. I was under huge pressure, but I think it was largely my own doing. The professor told me to go and seek help. He thought I was having a nervous breakdown at the time. And friends said I probably was." Instead of seeking help to cope with the system and fit in with the new direction of the department, Barry resigned. "The decision to resign was difficult, although it was remarkably easy at the time. Handing in the notice was almost like an act of bravado, and people were saying, don't do it, don't do it. In went the letter, and I got back the acknowledgement, and I thought, that's it."

Leaving his lecturing job was "not the first time that something like that happened". Barry grew up in England and joined the Royal Air Force at age 16, against the wishes of his father, a socialist postman. "I loved aircraft, and I made explosives and rockets and things — very interesting things that flew — and that's why I went to the air force. But when I got in there, it killed the interest completely — nothing to do with aircraft there, but to do with the military. I found this very unjust, the pointless discipline, having to do church parades for the royalty and attend church — I'm an atheist. I just had to get out, but I was signed up for 12 years, and they wouldn't let me out. I got out by deliberately antagonising them and putting them in a position where they really didn't require my services." He had communist literature sent to him. "The parcels arrived and of course they were sent off straight away to Special Branch or whatever and that was that. You couldn't be a possible communist and stay in the air force. I said, I'm not a communist, I'm just interested." Eventually, they discharged him.

Barry loved the charter work he did with his boat, a Galway hooker, after leaving UCD. It didn't bother him that it didn't make him a huge income. He was content to earn "enough to keep me going, and then stop". However, this way of life took him away from his children every summer for long periods, and his earnings were all going to a childminder. "It was completely pointless," he says. "And then there was the grief of not actually being with the children. My worst year was when Beannán was five. I was working out of Bantry and Baltimore, and I saw very little of him that summer. And I knew that Lucy was missing me. She said to me, 'Why don't you stay at home, why do you have to keep going away?' and I thought, 'Why? I don't have to.' It was that, really — the realisation that that's not the way to have a family."

Barry and Finola decided that, since her business is able to provide a sufficient income for the family now, Barry would stay at home. He describes the decision as "probably as important as the UCD resignation". Barry also has a range of practical skills, and is able to do construction work on their home. "Luckily, we got the cottage for very little and we don't have a massive mortgage. It's very small, essentially two rooms, with bedrooms in the attic. I'm in the process of extending that. It's all part of the same thing, you know, I wouldn't get involved in a big mortgage."

Barry describes himself as a minimalist. He dislikes cars and learned to drive only a few years ago. He walks or cycles whenever it's practical. "I'm not against cars; I'm against their overuse. I will walk if it's walkable — I'll walk six or seven miles." He feels that too many possessions can force people to maintain punishing ways of working, just to maintain a certain lifestyle and level of possessions. But he will spend money on things that are important to him. For their home extension, he and Finola "will have good stuff. We'll spend money on things we like, because it is a home. I don't regard that as possessions; we're not going to fill it with superfluous things — we'll furnish it aesthetically. I think we can stand back a bit and say, what do we sacrifice to maintain good standards in our home? We both have the same sort of values. We don't clash much over what we like." He says that Finola is, like himself, "fairly immune from consumerist culture. I think the things we have in common are probably the essential things, that is, non-dependence on the forces of the system."

"Being with the kids is brilliant. There's been a huge difference in them this summer," Barry says. "They're much happier just to sort of mess around the house and not want to do things. I suppose it's having somebody there all the time. Lucy had a great relationship with her childminder's family, so it's almost like repossessing. But it's easy to lapse. Even in the immediate situation, like the children fighting over something — how do you negotiate this so that you're not just somebody that solves the problem but a negotiator? Parents have to be pretty much negotiators. It is constant compromise and that is so difficult for me in a way."

Even though his chartering did not bring in much income, he also finds it hard to depend on Finola for money. "It's my choice, but nevertheless there's a great psychological need to be independent. And it's probably not a case of saying — just go to the account and draw from that — you have to earn the contribution. And that's part of the disease of the way we live. Even though I've attempted to change, I still sort of know I'm held there, by this need to be the earner. And thinking — the next few years — is this it? As a male, I'm not used to being in this position. Before, I could relate to it, but not as a person. Now I can see that there must be so many women putting in huge amounts of work."

Barry points out that capitalism requires that children be raised in a certain way. "Rearing kids is part of the whole capitalist enterprise to make integrated individuals. It's so integral to ideology," he says. But he also feels that children can learn to question convention, and he wants to be involved in the education of his own children. "I hope they don't become swamped by the necessities of earning a living or structuring a career, doing well. I'd hate to have a child who turned out to be a stockbroker — it would be so sad not to like your own child. That is pointless. So I think you have to make the effort, once you have children, to try and compromise. That's another thing. I'm self-educated — I left home when I was young and had a not very good academic record — I came round to study through correspondence schools. And I was very successful academically, after that. But that also has a lot to do with the way I'm bringing up my kids. I put an emphasis and a value on education, but it has to come from the individual."

For Barry, every choice carries regret for all the other possibilities he has turned down. Leaving the air force and leaving UCD were similar experiences for him, putting him in a sort of "orphan state". Both institutions were like a "large family with some sort of direction. After UCD, I had to force myself to say, look, you've done it now, stick with this. You have to ask how much do you depend on the environment psychologically. I do know a lot of people who have the same values, lifestyles, lack of ambitions, and they are my normal environment now. But I've missed the research, the intellectualising, an awful lot. I still carry on doing esoteric things at home. On and off I blitz maths for a couple of months. Or I just read. When I left UCD, I left behind a lot of my intellectual friends. That's the thing that I do miss most, the big regret that I have, that I lost that in a way, and I should really have maintained contact with very interesting friends."

If the family needs money in the future, Barry will sell his boat, but would find it difficult, as it has been such a big part of his life. "I have this long-term plan to import wine — take three people down to Bordeaux for not very much money a week, just a nominal charge. I bring back a cargo of wine, and they bring back some for themselves. You can make money, enough money, certainly, for me to go through the year on that with, say, four trips. I think in those terms — that's enough money, now I can do what I want. But I never sit down and do nothing. I'm always doing something, but it's work I *want* to do."

ॐ ॐ ॐ

Kate Mullaney and Marcus McCabe:
Back to the Land with Permaculture

Kate Mullaney and Marcus McCabe live in County Monaghan, Marcus' home place, with their three children, Tyrone, known as Toto (10), Róisín (8) and Casper (3). Marcus trained as a horticulturalist, and Kate as an archaeologist. Eight years ago, they started developing an eight-acre site, which they call The Ark, according to permaculture principles.[3] They have built a straw-bale house on the site, as well as a timber-framed barn, from where they run a business that supplies kits for reed-bed sewage systems. The barn also serves as a base for courses in permaculture, and a place to work with groups who come to study reed beds and other aspects of sustainable development.

The couple could be described as eco-pioneers. Their circular straw-bale house is built entirely from environment-friendly materials and has a thatch roof. They have a compost toilet and for health reasons do not use any aerosols, soaps or commercial cleaning agents, using instead washing soda, alcohol and vinegar. They wear natural fabrics, and produce as much of their own food as possible, all of it organic. In addition to their ecological commitments, the couple had home births for their children, do not inoculate them, and school them at home. Until recently, they hoped to develop an eco-village on the site with like-minded people. This plan eventually fell through, primarily for financial reasons, according to Marcus.

They now make a comfortable living from the reed-bed business, but have followed a road on which they sometimes had very little money. They lived in Dublin at first, after they met in 1990. Marcus had always been interested in organic horticulture and agriculture, but after college, he took a teach-

---

[3] Permaculture is a design philosophy and a philosophy for life, which aims to create systems that provide for human needs, using natural elements and drawing inspiration from natural ecosystems. It examines how to grow food, build houses, create communities, and minimise environmental impact.

ing job in a conventional horticultural college. He gave this up, however, because organics was ignored in that system. "Maybe if I'd had more patience, I could have stuck it out, stayed in the system and got things going," he says. "But I just didn't have the patience for it at the time. I was just teaching everybody how to spray this and spray that. What I was teaching basically consisted of — if you're growing raspberries, you use this spray and that spray. It was basically a spray programme."

Marcus worked for a time for various environmental organisations, after giving up his teaching job. Then, through the Centre for Alternative Technology in Wales, they discovered permaculture. "It opened everything up for me," Kate says. They took some courses in permaculture and decided that they would get out of Dublin and put it into practice on the land.

Around the time that Kate became pregnant with Toto, they went to Offaly, to a friend who had land and was hoping to start an eco-village. However, it became clear that the eco-village would not happen, and when Toto was eight months old, they moved to Fermanagh, just a few miles from where they now live, to a house that had been in Marcus' family for several generations. Marcus earned some money from forestry work, and other bits and pieces. By this stage, they were developing plans for a permaculture centre on a site on Marcus' parents' farm, and looking for sources of financial support. They secured a grant from the County Development Board and a loan from LEADER, which is now paid off, in order to buy the land and set up The Ark. With the money, they built polytunnels for cultivating reeds, along with the barn and the infrastructure for the reed-bed kits.

Until October 2000, they operated as sole traders, but then decided to become a company, which has made a big difference to their financial peace of mind. "From our experience, when you're a sole trader, you're so connected to the thing," says Kate. "It's *our* bank account, *our* phone bill, everything. And with a company, it's not like that any more. *It* pays the bills. And you can walk away at the end of the day. It really is liberating. And I think, as a result of that, the business has become more abundant and busier." They also find it a real boon to have the business on the same site as their home. Kate does most of the housekeeping, but Marcus is always available. "I can stop by here anytime. I can come over here and cook a meal," he says. "Men often went away from the home to work, but I'm close to it."

Once the business was established, they started to build their house, living in the barn while they did so. They did a lot of the labour themselves, but also employed expert trades people. "I think," says Marcus, "unless you're a very handy person, and have plenty of money, you need people with experience. Otherwise, you'll make a mess of the materials." They paid for the house by building in stages when money was available and have no mortgage.

When they first started work on The Ark, and especially when they were building the house, they found that they rarely took days off. As Kate explains, "We used to just take days off when a certain work or thing had finished. And then you'd find that friends or family would come at weekends and want our attention, and it would drive us crazy. Then we stood back and realised what we were doing. You know, we were putting a wall up, saying, do not come when we are doing whatever, be it Saturday or Sunday. We would never, ever stop. And then we thought, well, everyone takes a break on Saturday and Sunday, or at least on Sunday. We realised then that we had to, and it was a good thing really."

"When you're involved with your own place, it's never finished," adds Marcus. "There's always another door to be hung, or — like now, we're planning our greenhouse. Even though for ten years we've been talking about it — the lean-to greenhouse against the permaculture house — it never actually happened; we've never been able to afford one. Now, we can do it and we're really excited about that. It's going to make a huge difference to the house."

Marcus says that initial reactions to the house were incredulous. "The compost toilet is a big issue; I think it challenges people. But a lot of people accept it, because when they actually use the toilet, they realise it's fine. And when they see the steaming hot compost, that always impresses them. At some gut level, they know it's been treated very well. If you go to a septic tank, you see all the faeces in it, marinating away, and just downstream of the septic tank, you've got this horrible dangerous place. We don't have one of those dangerous places here — practically every other house in the country does and below every sewerage works as well. When you're talking to engineers about it, of all the different people you talk to, they're the least horrified by the idea of compost toilets, because they know the amount of civil works that goes into treating water, and they still can't get it right. So taking the solids out, not putting them in the water in the first place, makes an awful lot of sense to them."

Marcus is messianic in his enthusiasm and commitment to their way of life. Kate, while equally committed and uncompromising, finds it tedious to always be the pioneer, telling people about alternatives, "providing information about the compost toilet or the home schooling or the home birthing, because people are so incredulous all the time. And that's my own fault; it's no bearing really on other people as such. But I probably influence people way more than I know, because they think, come on, I never thought about that. And that's a good thing, to open people up to that information."

Marcus laughingly says that some people treat him almost "like the green priest going around". He continues, "I was staying with friends in Paris and I missed my plane, I got the times mixed up and I had to go back to their flat. I arrived back and they opened the door and all the aerosols were out, back on the table — the stuff they had put away while I was visiting. I was horrified to think it. I mean, we drive a van and we burn lots of fuel and we're an awful long way from pure."

The Ark has become one of the places where sustainable-development activists and eco-practitioners gather a couple of times a year, to share ideas and experiences. They also have links with educational groups from all over the country, especially those studying sustainable development. This work takes a lot of their time, but they place a high value on it. They also employ local people, mostly on a casual basis, which is another means of spreading their ideas.

The kind of sustainable society they would like to see is possible only on a bioregional or national basis, says Marcus. They are pragmatic and understand that it is practically impossible to live outside the mainstream system and that self-sufficiency within the present system is not viable. "When you choose to live alternatively, you think, I could make cheese, I could make my own clothes and I could make my own material," says Kate. "It's not because you feel you have to, it's because you're opened up to all these traditional crafts that are easy, really do-able. But you end up being so busy. You just can't do everything." Nevertheless, they have challenged the dominant ways of doing things to a huge degree. Kate, Marcus and their family have put a huge amount of energy and emotional commitment into creating a viable, environment-friendly and sustainable way of living. Having invested so much of themselves in The Ark, they intend to be there for a long time.

Conclusions

Many of these long-timers have an enduring commitment to creating alternative ways to live. They have always thought "outside the box" and while they did not all start out with definite plans for their lives, they responded to circumstances in creative and mindful ways, and continue to do so. Nóirín and Doc, who feature in Chapters Four and Five respectively, also belong to the category of long-timer. In establishing their ways to live from relatively early in adulthood, they did not have the cushions of redundancy lump sums or pensions. Doc now has the long-term security of his pension, and Laragh has her property, but early in their lives they could not have anticipated these securities. They and the other long-timers are very good at creative frugality and living within their means. In spite of the uncertainties they sometimes experience, they feel that they have the resources to cope with the unexpected in their lives, and the means to shape them. This feeling of a certain control is closely associated with happiness and well-being, according to Robert E. Lane's extensive research on happiness.

They are all involved with work that is important to them. Sometimes it is paid and sometimes not. They occupy a variety of roles, including those of artist, parent, grandparent, activist, carer, teacher, intellectual, designer, traveller, learner, and many more. Their lives are complex and demand the juggling of roles, and deadlines sometimes impose stress. Several work very hard, but for the most part they avoid becoming overburdened, so they are able to attend to all of their roles and responsibilities. Like the downshifters, they have decided on their priorities, and have designed their lives around those priorities, rather than just letting life happen to them.

Chapter Nine

LIVE WELL ON LESS MONEY

Many of us *will* need to learn to live with less money, if we are serious about having more time to enjoy life, to pursue passions or interests, to spend more quality time with friends or family, or to study or travel, or live up to our visions in any number of ways. We live in a work–earn–spend culture, which is also increasingly one of borrowing and credit. Few of us were taught to be critical of this culture, either at school or in our families.

This chapter provides ideas for cutting expenditure, so that ultimately you need to do less paid work, and have more time for your life's work and purpose. It complements the ideas in Chapter Six on developing financial intelligence and maximising your income from paid work. Its ideas are also inseparable from the project of cutting back on paid work, in order to create more time in your life, which is something that money cannot buy. By reducing your expenses and outgoings, you need to earn less, you therefore need less paid work, and you create more time in your life.

It is not my intention to be prescriptive about what you should do, only to give you some ideas that may make your vision of balance easier to achieve. Many of us spend without serious consideration of our needs and without reflecting on how well our purchases will serve us. Added to that, we often become dependent on spending as a way to solve problems, but this is a solution that fixes us even more firmly in a cycle that requires us to earn money.

This chapter is intended to serve as a means to develop the habit of mindful spending. The list of ideas is not comprehensive, but it will get you started. You can follow up on the ideas here by going to several good resources mentioned in the text and listed at the end of the book. Only you will know the meaning of mindful spending in your own life. But don't be too quick to dismiss all the ideas as inappropriate for your situation.

Eating In and Eating Out

We all eat on a daily basis and food is a major source of spending for everyone. We are typically so busy with our jobs that we regard food as just another product to consume. But eating well has links to both individual health and environmental health. If we are healthy, it keeps down medical bills. If our food is produced with minimum impact on the environment, it keeps down the cost of dealing with pollution from transport or the disposal of packaging, for example. Don't let the cheaper price of some foods fool you. Much inferior food has a lower price, which does not reflect the medical and planetary costs (which we all bear), and is not actually cheaper at all. It's important to distinguish between the *cost* of food and the *price* of food.

Many of the suggestions below require time. But they are also enjoyable, and many of them are sociable. If you are cutting back on the time spent at paid work, you will have the time to cook and shop in ways that keep your costs down.

Obvious ways to cut costs

- Avoid convenience foods and cook from scratch.

- Plan weekly menus and shop accordingly.

- Bulk-buy frequently used long-life staples such as flour, rice, beans, pulses and spices.

- Make a list before you go food shopping and stick to it.

- Join a food co-operative or start one (see *Resources*).

- Eat less meat. Replace it with beans or pulses on a couple of days a week. Buy dried pulses and beans, which are much cheaper than tinned.

- Be creative in your cooking. Invent recipes using what is in your cupboards, rather than go shopping for new ingredients.

- Bring packed lunches to work, rather than buying sandwiches or going to a restaurant on a regular basis. Ask your employer to install a microwave and kettle, if you don't already have those facilities. Use your office canteen if you like the food, and if the prices are favourable.

- Do you really need to pick up a coffee on your way to work? It's very expensive for what you get. Why not make some when you get there, using a Fairtrade[4] brand?

- Take a picnic when you go out with children. Restaurant food is very expensive and children often don't eat all they get.

- For special occasion wining and dining, be prepared to spend a little more on eating at home, as an alternative to eating out. It is always less costly, and you will probably be able to afford nicer wines than you could in a restaurant.

Cutting environmental costs

- Buy local food in season. This is less costly in terms of price and environment, as it is not transported a long way. It is also likely to be fresher, and not to have been irradiated or artificially ripened, which is better for your health. Read Helena Nordberg Hodge's article, "The Case for Local Food".

- Buy organic. Food may have a higher price per item, but it is better for your health, it is produced in ways that do not harm

---

[4] Fairtrade products are produced under a partnership between producers and consumers, which ensures that producers receive a fair price for the work they do (see *Resources*).

the environment, and its flavour is much better, meaning that a little goes a long way.

- Avoid GM (genetically modified) products. The GM process inserts the genes from one species to another, in order to produce different characteristics, such as resistance to disease. But it causes irreversible damage to ecosystems.

- Avoid supermarkets as much as possible. As supermarket chains grow, their power forces farmers to accept low prices. This means that farmers have to cut costs, often resulting in very poor farming practices, especially where animals are concerned. The power of the large chains also means that they source food from developing countries where they can use cheap labour and where pollution-control laws do not exist, or can be ignored. In addition, the average item you buy in a supermarket has travelled 1,000 miles and transport pollution is the largest single cause of global warming.

- Support box delivery services for organic vegetables, as well as country markets. This helps the local economy in your community and avoids transport costs, which include pollution. Buying locally produced organic food also makes it financially viable for local growers to produce it.

- Buy Fairtrade tea, coffee, sugar, chocolate, cocoa, honey, bananas and other products. You will know that the people who produced them have received a fair price and had fair working conditions.

Eating Out

There are no hard and fast rules about eating out. It is nice sometimes and there are mindful ways to do it. Like everything else that you spend your money on, you have to judge if it is worth the life energy that it costs.

- Why not go out for breakfast or lunch? You will be able to do this if your work is more flexible. Both are cheaper options than eating out in the evening and lunch menus are often similar to dinner menus.

- Support your local restaurants, rather than chains, for the same reasons as you support local markets and shops and avoid supermarkets.

- Before you go, be clear with your companions about who is paying for what. Too often, at the end of a meal, someone suggests splitting the bill evenly among all present. People on a budget can find themselves paying more than they anticipated and, at that stage, it can be difficult to object.

Consider Your Car Usage

As well as being the biggest source of pollution today, the car is also a huge drain on our finances. Avoid borrowing for car purchase. Cutting down on car usage can save you money and improve your health, as well as making your environment cleaner and quieter. As well as considering the ideas below, read *Cutting Your Car Use*, by Anna Semlyen.

- Sell one of the cars in your household.

- Use public transport, walking and cycling as much as possible and use your car only for essential journeys.

- Start a car pool with other commuters on your route.

- When you take your car out, do as many tasks as possible on the one trip.

- Drive as small a car as possible, in order to minimise tax and insurance costs.

- Make your existing car last as long as possible before replacing it.

- Find out the most cost-effective speed for your car to run at.

- Learn to do routine maintenance yourself.

- Anticipate major repairs and services, and make sure you do your research to get the best value for them. Shop around for a reliable local mechanic before you need one.

- Get rid of your car and hire one when you need to.

- Investigate car-sharing with friends or starting a car-sharing club (see *Short Circuit*, by Richard Douthwaite and *Cutting Your Car Use*, by Anna Semlyen).

Cut Housing Costs

Housing is also an issue for everyone. It is the biggest expense by far for the average family. In Ireland, it is generally considered essential to own one's home. Many also succumb to the "more is better" mentality in regard to housing and aim to trade up regularly. Renting is regarded as a waste of money. It is considered "logical" that one should buy, because of the tax relief available on mortgages. Renting, however, also qualifies for tax relief now, and without the disadvantage of debt.

Don't be pressurised into buying, simply because our culture suggests that home-owning is a ticket to respectability. Lending institutions now lend a much greater percentage of the cost of a house than they used to, but this does not mean that they are in the business of making your dreams come true, as their advertising suggests. Their primary goal is to maximise profit for their shareholders. If you do decide to buy, don't buy more house than you can afford. Calculate just how much you can afford in monthly repayments, including insurance, and taking any other debts into account also. In the short term, lending agencies may put people in the "home of their dreams", but in the long term, the high repayments mean that borrowers are tied to highly stressful lifestyles.

Most of the people featured in this book live in modest-sized homes, placing a high value on comfort and aesthetically pleasing surroundings. Several used lump sums from redundancies or early retirement packages to pay off mortgages. Richard Douthwaite has never had a mortgage and his adult children are also saving in order to build homes without mortgages. Laragh Neelin has avoided mortgages almost completely, having had a very small one for only three years. Those who have mortgages keep them as small as possible. Mortgage is a form of long-term debt, although this is often overlooked, and it is financially wise to pay it off as quickly as possible.

Some of those you have met are content to rent, seeing it as the best solution for their current needs. In many European countries, about 70 per cent of the population rent their homes. Britain and Ireland are unusual in the emphasis on ownership. If you plan to travel in the future, or you want to work in different parts of the country, or if you do not want to take on the long-term debt of a mortgage, then renting may well meet your needs better than buying. If you act with integrity as a tenant, you will usually find that landlords treat you with integrity also. Also read John O. Anderson's article, "Why We Prefer to Rent".

Undoubtedly, though, reform of the private rental sector is long overdue. Rental costs are very high, go uncontrolled, and tenants have no security of tenure. You could consider campaigning for legislative reform, if you find yourself with time, having cut back on your job time. (See *Resources* for details of housing associations and reform campaigns.)

Like all other aspects of balanced living, there are no blueprints for housing. Below, I suggest some ways to think differently about where and how to live. Some of them are illustrated in the stories in this book. Others are the solutions of other people I met as I researched this book, although their full stories do not feature. The *Resources* section contains details of special schemes or organisations mentioned.

- Rent out rooms or a room in your house, in order to help with your mortgage if you have one, or to create income, if you have no mortgage.

- If you have a holiday home, rent it out while you are not using it.

- If you go away for long periods, rent out your home while you are away.

- Move to a smaller house.

- Move to an area where house prices are lower.

- Move to an apartment.

- "House sit" or caretake homes for people who are away.

- Work as a live-in carer for children, an old person, someone with a disability or an invalid, in return for free housing.

- Buy a boat to live on.

- Buy a small piece of land and camp there or live in a mobile home, while building. There are still parts of the country where sites are affordable. You can build in stages, when you have money.

- Join or start a housing co-operative or housing association.

- Consider shared ownership with a local authority. This will help you get on the mortgage ladder, if that is what you want. And you can sell your share of the property if and when you want.

Some of these solutions may take courage. Our culture encourages us to judge people according to their homes, and it may not be easy to trade "down", or to rent, in the knowledge that others may not understand your reasons, or may pity you.

Holidays

Earn-and-spend lifestyles encourage us to spend a lot on holidays. Many people overspend on them, resulting in personal debt. In addition, we frequently travel to our destinations by airplane, which is a huge cause of global warming. Add to that the way in which foreign venues are being "developed" and local cultures are being commodified in the name of tourism, and the cost to the planet for holidays is also high.

As your life becomes more balanced, you will be less tired because your work life is in control. You will find yourself generally happier and more mindful about your spending, and you will need fewer holidays away from home. You may also enjoy being around your home on your time off work. You will have time to enjoy it, to garden if you have a garden, to entertain friends, and to make excursions to galleries, theatres and other amenities close to home. Seeing familiar things, people and places with new eyes can be as much of an adventure as travel to exotic lands and a search for places that other tourists have not yet discovered. Your adventures in balance will not poison the atmosphere, damage the environment or exploit other people.

When you do travel, you may choose your destinations more carefully and appreciate them more. You will have the time to research the best price and the sort of experience most in line with your values. You will also be able to get much more pleasure from travel, because you won't be under pressure to prove that you are doing well by taking an expensive holiday, you won't feel under pressure to enjoy the limited time you have for the holiday, and you won't feel cheated when it doesn't turn out as advertised.

You may travel at your leisure, and enjoy getting to your destination, perhaps using more environmentally friendly transport like walking, cycling, trains, buses and boats. You will have time to get to know people, maybe doing paid or unpaid work in various places. Why not consider doing voluntary work with an organisation that you support? You might take a camping holiday, either alone or with friends or family. Whatever creative option you decide on, it will probably cost a lot less than the all-inclusive packages that many spend-and-earn people now take.

Spend Mindfully

The most effective way to minimise spending is not to shop. Don't go to shopping malls, don't browse internet stores, don't pick up mail order catalogues indiscriminately, simply because you have nothing better to do. When you do spend, do it mindfully, not in response to an impulse.

I could add many more categories to the suggestions for cutting outgoings, such as running your home, clothing, accessories, entertainment and sports equipment. But the same principles apply to all spending. If you know how many hours it has taken you to earn the money for an item or service, then you can make a properly informed decision about whether it is worth the price. Spending mindfully is not about saying a blanket "no" to possessions, but about considering how they can serve you, and how much space, time and effort they will take up in your life.

Before buying something, remind yourself that you are spending your life energy. Then ask yourself the following questions. All of the questions apply to things and some of them apply to services. The list is combined from questions suggested by FI (Financial Independence) Associates and Jacqueline Blix and David Heitmiller in their book *Getting a Life*.

I suggest that the questions in the first group are fundamental, and should apply to every purchase.

1. Do I need it?

2. How many do I already have?

3. How much will I use it?

4. How long will it last?

5. Can I borrow it from a friend or family member?

6. Is there anything I already own that I can substitute for it?

7. Can I do without it?

8. Will I have to go without something else, which I need more, if I buy this?

9. Would I buy this if I had to pay cash?

10. Have I researched it to get the best quality for the best price?

11. Do I know my current credit card balance?

12. Can I buy this on credit and clear the debt this month?

13. Am I able to clean, lubricate and/or maintain it myself?

14. Am I willing to?

15. Will I be able to repair it?

16. If I can't or won't repair or maintain it myself, how much will those services cost me?

The second group encourages you to think a bit more about your desire for something.

17. Will my life be very negatively affected if I don't buy this?

18. Am I buying this because I'm depressed or bored?

19. Could I feel better now without spending money? How?

20. If I wait a day or a week and come back, will I still want it?

The questions below connect your purchase to the environment and to the people who produced your prospective purchase.

21. How will I dispose of it when I'm finished with it?

22. Was anybody exploited while this was being produced?

23. Are the resources that went into it renewable or non-renewable?

24. How far did this travel, and what effects did that have on the environment?

25. Is it made of recycled material and is it recyclable?

Mindful spending is not about self-denial. It requires that we think about how our possessions serve us, but it is not about feeling that we must give them up. Duane Elgin quotes Mahatma Gandhi: "As long as you derive inner help and comfort from anything, you should keep it. If you were to give it up in a mood of self-sacrifice or out of a stern sense of duty, you would continue to want it back, and that unsatisfied want would make trouble for you. Only give up a thing when you want some other condition so much that the thing no longer has any attraction for you."

The principles of mindful spending also apply to self-help books, even this one. Get your local library to order the books you want to read. If, having read one, you think your life would be enhanced if you owned it, then buy. But remember that, once you have grasped the basic principles, it is usually more productive to do something, and in the process to work out your own variations, rather than buy another book. Be careful too about costly seminars or workshops. It can be very helpful to explore issues of balance in the company of other people, but don't let that become a substitute for the real thing — personal action.

De-commercialise Rituals

Even for the most determined, most creative and happiest practitioner of mindful spending, it can be hard to resist the pressures to spend at Christmas. Many of us go along with it, in spite of our better judgement, because questioning the culture of spending in a family or group of friends can cause so much trouble. Most people say that they disagree with the over-commercialisation of Christmas, but still find it hard to reduce spending and gift-giving in their personal lives.

If you are communicating with friends and family about your choices, you should be able to gradually make changes. Suggest spending limits on gifts, and limits on the number of gifts. If you buy, try to ensure that your purchases are fairly traded, or that the proceeds from them go to a cause that you support. Try spending time together as an alternative to gift giving. Make decorations, gifts and cards. Prepare simple food to eat at home, rather than eating out or buying convenience foods. Of course, all of this takes time, and you may be creating more time in your life, but those around you may not be, so they will still feel the need to spend, in order to compensate. But gradually, changes can take place. Many simple living groups and websites suggest alternative, non-commercial ways to celebrate Christmas.

Likewise, weddings are a source of enormous spending, and another opportunity to compete in the spending stakes. Gift lists at department stores and the search for stunning clothes are part of it for the guests. Resist the pressures to go along with the formula. For couples, diamonds have been promoted as symbols of eternal love for quite some time. We also have dedicated magazines and dressmakers for the worn-once dress and, more recently, wedding consultants. The meaning of the commitment being entered in marriage is often lost in the commercialisation. If you are getting married, why not try to devise a simple celebration, which reflects the importance of your relationship? It's also very easy to forget the reason for celebrating such events as christenings, holy communions and confirmations. As with weddings, a commitment is being entered into and this is often forgotten in the rush to celebrate commercially.

Funerals are another source of spending. We feel under pressure to have the most expensive coffin, or other accessories, in order to show our respect to the deceased. Mourners often spend a lot of money on flowers, often imported and hothouse-grown using pesticides. Why not have family flowers only, preferably home-produced, and keep everything else as simple as possible?

Birthdays have also become increasingly commercialised in recent years. Does the child's party have to be celebrated with a home entertainer, a party that you pay for at the local leisure centre or a trip to McDonald's? The pressures to organise activities like these are strong. Talk to other parents about alternatives, as it is very difficult to resist by yourself. But you can resist; and you may be surprised at the relief other parents express, and their willingness to help devise games and activities that don't cost a fortune. Adults have birthdays too, of course and if you are celebrating yours or planning for a partner's birthday, it's worth thinking about what you really want from the celebration, and using the principles of mindful spending to achieve it.

Think Creative Frugality

As you explore ways to minimise spending, maximise time and bring quality into your life, you can also explore the concept of frugality. You might not like the term, associating it with poverty and penny-pinching, but actually it is an elegant and creative way of expressing the importance of quality over quantity, according to Joe Dominguez and Vicki Robin. It is intricately linked with the concept of *enough*, not just in terms of spending less or having fewer possessions, but also in a wise use of our life energy.

Frugality means that you don't have to prove yourself in any way, by means of what you *have*. It requires a different approach, which is oriented at helping us to *be* more. The key to balanced consumption is to spend mindfully, focusing on high-quality durable items that you really want. In this way, you can escape the work–earn–spend cycle. The people you have met in this book are clear about this. Whether they have a lot of money or a little, they do not use possessions to prove anything, either to themselves or to other people. They place a lot more emphasis on the people they are with and what they are doing, than on what they are wearing, driving, or using as an accessory.

Balanced consumption is about realising that just because we can afford something, it doesn't follow that we ought to buy it. It means not buying it if you don't need it. By consuming less, we use fewer resources, and we help to reduce the gap between rich and poor, both locally and internationally. Being happy with enough means that there is more to go round. And the good news is that if we consume less, we need less money, we need to do less paid work, we have more time for our life's work, and balance can make its way into our lives. Creative frugality, in other words, can give us the things that money cannot buy.

Frugality, derived from a sense of enough, also helps us to create our own micro-economics, which gives us confidence in our ability to cope with the future. Frugality teaches us to plan, which allows us to maximise any financial opportunities that come our way. But it also teaches us that excessive worry about money is destructive. It gives us the resources to live happily with what we have in the present. This sense of confidence is central to happiness. Be patient with yourself, however. By cultivating a frugal mindset, you are changing the infrastructure of your life, as Jacqueline Blix and David Heitmiller explain. So it may take time

— six months, a year, two years or more. But remember, this is just a fraction of the time you could spend trapped in a work–earn–spend cycle.

Communicate with Those around You

When you seriously take steps to balance your life and escape the work–earn–spend cycle, you are bucking the system, and that can be a lonely journey. Few people talk openly about their finances, nor do they understand what their money attitudes are, or where they come from. As you explore these issues and their effects on your life, talk to other people close to you. If you have a life partner, it is especially important, whether or not you operate joint finances, but particularly if you do. Don't talk in a spirit of blame, trying to find out who is responsible for money difficulties. Dominguez and Robin's mantra on this is "no shame, no blame". Take the attitude that you are talking in order to come up with solutions, including ways to maximise income and minimise outgoings. Help each other to control spending.

Your family of origin has its own culture concerning money and material goods. Unspoken expectations concerning spending, celebrations, gifts and outings exist in every family. It can be extremely difficult to go against the grain with parents, siblings and extended family; if consumerism goes unquestioned, possessions are seen as a mark of success, job titles and high earnings bring status, and expensive gifts and celebrations are seen as a mark of esteem. Consumerist practices have the "patina of public acceptability", in the words of Mark Burch. Take small steps in your efforts to communicate your new thinking about work and money.

Don't stop at talking to those in your family. Be honest with friends about what you are trying to do. If you are going out for a meal or drinks, this can be a good opportunity. You can bring up the subject by clarifying beforehand how much you want to spend and who pays for what. Don't expect that they will begin to think about the concept of enough overnight. But don't let that put you off. Then look for other people who are already enjoying practising a philosophy of enough. Chances are, you already know some, but have not seen them in this way before. Maybe you dismissed them as unambitious or unsuccessful in conventional terms, because they seemed unconcerned with status and material possessions. Talk to them too and see what you can learn. Many people are working on the concept of enough, as a means to achieve wellbeing and balance, but most are not passing it on publicly, or getting media attention, or even thinking of it as a formal philosophy. We need to create a culture where these issues are seen as important, and where knowledge regarding them can be shared.

If you work with other people on putting your thoughts into practice, as a group you can make conspicuous consumption seem ostentatious and balanced living seem the norm in that group. You can discuss spending limits on gifts. You can talk to other parents about limiting TV watching — your own and your children's. You might even work with other people in your community (your street, church group or parents' association, if you have children at school) to agree not to buy expensive clothing, runners and so on for your children. Discussing these things in groups and working with others leads to better outcomes for everyone. It also means that we merge our personal visions with those of a group or community in a spirit of equality and mutual respect. The section on learning groups or study circles in Chapter Ten might also interest you.

Chapter Ten

USING TIME WISELY IN YOUR BALANCED LIFE

Only you can decide how to use your time, once you have used the philosophy of enough to help you escape the work–earn–spend cycle. You can do the things you have always wanted to do, but not had the time for, like educating yourself, writing, gardening, travelling, drama, learning languages, exercising, reading, playing music, making things, being a good friend and family member, working in your communities of interest and your local community, being creative and politically active. In short, you can live.

If you have been used to having a job to structure your life, it can be a bit frightening if you find yourself with responsibility for scheduling your own time. If you are balancing your life, you won't be tired on your time away from paid work, so it won't be a question of sleeping and recovering during time off. It's probably best to plan your time, at least loosely. Don't allow trivia to fill up your days. Make appointments with yourself or other people, or structure your days around some planned activity. But don't become inflexible. One of the nicest things about having time is that it allows you to be open to unexpected opportunities. The following sections look at some of the things you could start to cultivate and that add cumulatively to balance and happiness.

Health

It is difficult to feel happy when you are not feeling well. You would do well to invest some of your time in looking after your health, by taking gentle exercise and following a balanced diet.

You will have time to cook high-quality, nutritious and delicious food. You will have time to share meals with friends and, in general, to eat in a relaxed way that adds to the enjoyment of your food. You will have time for exercise, but won't become obsessive about it, and won't feel guilty when you don't do it, understanding that the body also benefits from rest. You will have time to get to understand your body and its cycles, and not feel the need to treat it like a machine to be maintained.

Don't forget the importance of doing nothing and being lazy. We need to revive the term laziness in a positive way. It's not wasted time; it is essential for health, creativity and equilibrium. There will also be time to get plenty of sleep, which restores body and mind. You will have time for play and fun. Good mental health also arises from having connections in a community, from being heard, seen and known. When you have more time, you are able to spend more time developing relationships with other people, be they neighbours, relatives or people in interest groups or learning groups.

The Green Triangle

Physical health, financial health and environment are in a triangle, as Ernest Callenbach points out. Any time you do something beneficial for one of them, you almost inevitably do something beneficial for the other two, whether you intend to or not. And it doesn't matter at which point of the triangle you start. For example, if you take care of your health by eating less meat and dairy products, you will save money, since they are relatively expensive products, and you will help the environment, since meat and dairy production are land-intensive and a damaging use of farm resources. If you decide for environmental reasons to cycle or walk to work, you are also doing something for your health and your pocket. And any time you decide to save money by not buying a product that requires a lot of raw materials and an intensive production process, you are helping the earth. You are probably also doing your health a favour, because you don't have the stress of needing to earn the money to buy the product. By not having to use the product, in order to justify its purchase, you also save time and have more time for relationships, which in turn is good for your health. Avoiding debt is also a sure way to avoid worry, which in turn is detrimental to mental health.

Spirituality and Connectedness

The development of a spiritual dimension is also linked to health and happiness. Your spirit is your creative source of energy, which "reflects the moving force within the universe itself", in the words of Brian Thorne. Developing this sense of connection with a universal energy will also help you to understand that you are not isolated from other people and from the earth, but are a part of a greater whole. You need regular quiet time, in order to reflect on the meaning and purpose of your life and to develop your vision. You can also develop your spirituality through contact with nature, through meditation, or through religious practice.

Whatever way you choose to approach spirituality, I urge you to be open to it. When you are not pushed for time, you can listen to others when they mention it and seek to understand what they believe and why. You can really appreciate the natural world, either by being active in it or by contemplating it. Take time to watch birds, flowers, trees, animals, sunrises, stars, moonlight, and a host of other natural wonders that we often miss when we are hurried and dissatisfied.

Both individuality and connectedness are important in the development of good health and happiness. The physicist and philosopher Fritjof Capra has observed that through self-assertion the individual maintains the diversity and energy essential to the creative potential of the whole. Combining individuality with integration into a group or collective makes for a healthy system. Modern ways of living emphasise individualism and compartmentalisation. Devote time to your relationships, from the closest and most intimate, to those with relative strangers. Relationships thrive when people feel that they are heard and that those around them take the time to listen. When you have the time, you can invest it in listening, in modelling good relationship skills. Clearly, you cannot have the same degree of relationship with everybody, but that does not mean that every encounter cannot have good qualities.

Individuality is different from individualism, and a sense of connectedness is not the same as being bound by cultural norms. The Dalai Lama has said, "the aim of the awakening mind is two-fold — to attain enlightenment and to benefit all sentient beings". In broadening the sense of our connection to nature, to other people and to the world, and by developing our self-reflective consciousness, we can begin to become agents of change in our worlds, local and global.

Education

Time allows you to educate yourself throughout your life. Education is not just about gaining qualifications, although you will have time to pursue these, if you decide it's what you want. It involves becoming informed about the world around you, how it works, and what role you play in it. It is about becoming politically, socially and economically literate, asking questions about what is taken for granted and finding answers that address your concerns and doubts. Education helps you to think about the whole global system, and the long term, as well as your immediate situation in the here and now. This, combined with a sense of connection to the world around you, helps you to move beyond conventional expectations about work and success.

Education also helps you to be a critical media user. The short-term nature of consumerist thinking has "dumbed down" discussions in the media about the problems we face in creating well-being for everybody. You will have time to support the minority of programmes and articles that put forward alternative thinking on economics and politics. Write to the producers, editors and broadcasters expressing your support. Write letters to editors and if you feel confident enough, ring radio talk shows to discuss alternative viewpoints on work, the economy and quality of life.

You will have time to read good books. Academic books, novels and biography are all informative about alternatives to the mainstream. You will have time to join a reading circle that discusses the books. You can visit independent-media websites and discuss what you find there.

Because you have time, you will be able to create not only a better life for yourself and your immediate circle, but also to make a difference to the wider world around you. One of the best books available at the moment, about how to spend less, consume less and contribute towards saving the earth, is *Go MAD (Make a Difference)*, from *The Ecologist* magazine.

Wise Consumption

When you have more time, you also have the means to consume wisely, by seeking out local sources for goods and services. Local enterprises are human in scale and they keep money and jobs circulating in the local area, without sucking out profits for shareholders who live elsewhere. You can start up or support local non-monetary exchange systems such as LETS (Local Exchange Trading System), which trade without money, where you barter services and get to know other people (see *Resources*).

You can also take the time to seek out and buy in Fairtrade shops, which trade in foreign goods in a non-exploitative way. If you have money to invest, you can take the time to ensure that it is invested ethically. You can campaign to make sure that the full costs — environmental, human and social — of every product and every business decision are disclosed and that they are met by those who make the decisions.

Children, Time, Money and Happiness

A common response to the ideas in this book is that balance and breaking the work–earn–spend cycle are next to impossible when you have children. Yet other doubters say, it's okay for the downshifters who still have relatively good incomes, even if smaller than before. But a persistent idea is that those operating in the long term on low incomes are depriving their kids. And every-body says, wait until they become teenagers — the pressures will be insurmountable then. Of course, it is more complicated and expensive when you have financial responsibilities to others, than if you have to attend only to your own relationship with work and money. Yet for many people, their children are a motivating factor in the search for balance.

I have referred to children at other points in the book, but it is not primarily about children. This section is a fairly brief over-view of the main issues, and if you want to investigate them fur-ther, you would do well to start by reading *For Our Own Good: Childcare Issues in Ireland*, by Bernie Purcell, and Jacqueline Blix and David Heitmiller's excellent chapter, "Your Money or Your Child's Life" in their book, *Getting a Life*.

Start with yourself

One cannot begin to create a balanced life for children unless one thoroughly understands the issues surrounding balance in one's own life. You cannot help your children to be critical of consumer-ist values if you do not practise that critique yourself. You cannot create happiness and self-esteem for others if you don't under-stand them in your own life. You may have to examine your own past as a child also. Are you trying to make up to your kids with material goods what you didn't have yourself? If you are spend-ing time working on your life vision and thinking about your life purpose, and being honest with yourself about how you use your money and your time, this is the best way to work out how to deal with these issues in your children's lives.

We all want our children to have the best out of life, to have their material needs met and to have memorable experiences. We also want them to be successful and happy. However, defining success and achievement for our children is just as crucial as defin-ing it for ourselves. Instead of asking what we want for them, write Blix and Heitmiller, it would be better to ask what they need. Most of what children need cannot be bought. They need attention, affection, play, humour, guidance and conversation, all of which require time. They need safety as they explore the issues they need to understand, in order to make their way in the world. They need adults who are able to negotiate and reach decisions by consensus. This is an especially important process for children to learn early in life. It is a democratic way of behaving in any group, including families, but it is a time-consuming process that often gets sidelined in very busy lives.

Seeking balance does not imply that parents and only parents should care for their children. There is nothing intrinsically un-balanced about carefully using good crèches and other forms of non-parental childcare. But it is unbalanced to rely on them to the extent that you could not organise your life without them. And men — not just women — must start demanding and creating flexible work arrangements, to facilitate having more time for children. Children as young as three are able to understand the trade-off between spending on things and the pleasures of spend-ing time with you.

Children are prime targets for advertisers. Very early in their lives, they receive the message that you are what you own. Just as you need to be critical of advertising, you should give your chil-dren the skills to do the same. Emphasise what you are *doing* to-gether, rather than what you might be *buying*. When I interviewed Trish Hehir and Mícheál Ó Raghallaigh, I was particularly struck by Trish's description of a winter's afternoon in their kitchen. School and dinner were over, it was almost dark at about four o'clock, and the three older children and their parents were play-ing a board game together. Richard Douthwaite also described how the whole family used to get involved in helping daughter Lucy with her essays, when she was a student nurse. Times like these are invaluable.

If you are worried about depriving your children, consider Amy Dacyczyn's ideas on creativity. She says that you can substi-tute creativity for money in many of the things you do with chil-dren. "When there is lack of resourcefulness, inventiveness and innovation, thrift means doing without. When creativity combines with thrift, you may be doing it without money, but you are not doing without."

Children also need to learn what money is and how it works, say Blix and Heitmiller. They may see you write a cheque, or use a plastic card and receive goods or services in return. They don't automatically know that these represent money and that you exchange your life energy for money by doing paid work. Even more puzzling, they see you go to an ATM, push a few keys and get cash. It is good for them to learn to manage small allowances and to have savings from early in their lives. They need to learn that choices are available to all of us about how we use our money.

The concept of enough can provide a common language for families and children to talk about what they want from life. Don't look for perfection in your parenting because, as Bernie Purcell emphasises, you won't find it. Ask yourself what it means to be a good enough parent. If you limit expectations of yourself, you will also learn not to place pressure on your children, not to hurry them in their day-to-day movements and activities, their educational development, their speech development, their sports and so on.

Children also benefit from doing nothing, learning to daydream or amuse themselves by means of their imaginations. You can also do things together as a family or with another family, like walks, cycling, reading, playing with pets, or just having quiet time. Don't overload them with activities. Just as we need to guard against overload in ourselves, we need to ensure that our children are not overwhelmed by a constant round of lessons, sports and parties. Apart from the expense, it is often very stressful to manage the travel and organisation required.

Teenagers

Teenagers are particularly vulnerable to the "more is better" philosophy of a consumer lifestyle, and the constant pressure to compare themselves to others. But they too need to learn about the financial and credit traps that exist. Tell them about the ideas you are developing, and the ways you are beginning to see money in a different light. They can also be given responsibility for managing their allowances. For example, if you keep financial records for the family over a period of a year, you will have a good idea of how much is spent on a teenager's clothing. Through careful scrutiny of the record, you can also decide, in consultation with the teenager, but reserving the final decision for yourself, how much to make available for the coming year. Your son or daughter can then take charge of the allowance and buy for themselves, but in the understanding that you will not bail them out if they spend irresponsibly. You can use this technique with any goods, including sport equipment, computer software, and CDs.

You can also involve teenagers in the family accounts, so that they get a sense of what it costs to run a home. If you are doing your own monthly accounts and planning, there is no reason why every adult and teenager should not be involved. Then, when it comes to making decisions on something like a holiday, everyone can take part.

Peer Pressure

In the chapters on personal spending, I urged you to reflect on who is in your reference group, that is, the people to whom you compare yourself. Peer pressure affects all of us, not just children and teenagers. Jacqueline Blix and David Heitmiller have a section on peer pressure, which I have summarised as follows:

1. Make sure you are not guilty of "keeping up with the Joneses", and being constantly concerned about what other people think. If you cannot say "no" to yourself, it is difficult to justify saying "no" to your child.

2. Think about your child's environment. For example, if your children attend a fee-paying school in an affluent area, pressures will exist to keep up with the level of consumption of other children with regard to cars, holidays, accessories, electronic equipment and clothing. Your children are likely to mix with a more diverse group of peers if they go to a local public

school, where they will mix with people who have both more and less than they have.

3. Make sure your children spend time with people of all ages, not just their peers. Spending time with grandparents, aunts, uncles, cousins and friends of different ages, as well as adult friends, can help them broaden their frames of reference beyond their peer group.

4. Give them a broad range of experiences, so that they don't take their own affluence for granted. Take them with you when you go places beyond your own area. Discuss with them the differences they see in how people live, not just in other countries, but in places close to home. Encourage them to correspond with pen pals, read about other cultures and get to know people who have moved here from other parts of the world. Reading stories of children who have overcome adversity can also extend their horizons.

5. Monitor how much time your children spend watching television. Educate yourself and them about advertising and other media content and intent. Much of TV consists of sales pressure, and the more time they spend watching it, the more their concept of the world resembles that on TV. You can also help them to be discriminating viewers, and to watch educational, engaging programmes.

6. Be aware of your children's school environment. One of the big advantages of balancing your life is that it gives you the flexibility to be involved in their education. Get to know the teachers and keep lines of communication open. Take the initiative in this, if no home-school links programme exists already. Volunteer to help with classroom activities or trips. Talk to other parents. This is a good way to combat the "everyone else is doing it" syndrome, and you may well find other parents who are looking for alternatives.

7. Reserve the right of parental veto. You are, after all, responsible for them and their welfare. Negotiation should be the first

line of action, but don't be afraid to say no. But do explain the reasons for your decision.

Young Adult Children

As teenagers become young adults, the issues don't go away. It is commonly assumed that parents should finance education, cars, accommodation, and travel, to name but a few activities, for their young adult children. Blix and Heitmiller assert that only you can decide how you want to do this, and where to draw the line. You may want to make finances available in the form of loans or gifts. You may decide to do neither. You also need to ask yourself about your financial relationship with your own parents, when you were a young adult and in the present. What kind of expectations do you and did you have, and how are these influencing your relationship with your own adult children? What will you do if your children accumulate debt? How will you feel if they take your financial support for granted, given that, if you let them, they will almost always prefer to spend your money than to earn and spend their own? These questions blend into all the other themes of the book as a whole, and it is never too late for young adults to develop financial intelligence. If you can give them a head start from a young age, so much the better. But there comes a time when you are no longer responsible for them, and the best gift you can give them is a copy of *Your Money or Your Life*.

Some thoughts for the child-free

Even if you are not a parent, or if your children are grown up, you probably have contact with children, as aunt, uncle, cousin, grandparent, friend, teacher or club official, or through your job or your voluntary work. We are all responsible for the messages given to children in our society. Talk to them about the choices you make for balance. Be honest about the benefits and the difficulties of balanced living in consumer society. Discuss value for money with them. Do activities with them that don't cost a lot. Model ways of being successful and happy that do not always require spending or competing with others. Be careful when giving gifts not to sabotage their parents' efforts to make them financially responsible and intelligent. In short, continue to put balance into practice when you are with them.

Start a Study Circle or Learning Group

Another way to use time wisely is to take personal education and communication with individuals that bit further and start a study circle. Find like-minded people who can act as a support group and a forum for developing ideas and increasing understanding of the issues involved in the philosophy of enough. You may already be a member of a larger community, such as a church, a political party, or a group of co-workers, within which you could start a study circle. A small group could agree to meet once a week for six or eight weeks, to begin. The power of intentional groups to support individual efforts for change is well documented. As soon as you have moved beyond being merely intellectually curious about the concept of enough and have started putting it into practice in your life, however tentatively, you will have concrete experiences and questions that you can bring to a group. Groups can be creative sources for their members, and the concept of enough is one that lends itself readily to development in community with other people.

You may feel confident enough to take a leadership role in the group or you may engage someone else to act as a facilitator. There is no right way to achieve the changes you desire, but your first session could start with introductions of the group members, who also outline their interest in and experience of the issues surrounding enough. Then it is important to set ground rules for participation, which ensure that everybody has equal speaking time, and the right to be listened to, and to have personal information remain confidential. You can move on to sharing a range of views on the topic, summarising the common ground found during the discussions and, finally, evaluating the session and planning what to cover in the next sessions. It is usually wise to have modest aims for groups like these at the start. It may simply be enough to agree to provide support for each other in the effort to make changes in individual lifestyles.

Your group might eventually decide to hold a one-off workshop or seminar on the concept of enough. A well-designed workshop can stimulate community interest and spread the ideas. It is important in any workshop to avoid too many abstract ideas and to bring discussions to focus on realistic actions that people can take, as well as possible consequences of these actions. Adults are capable of being highly active in their learning process, given the right conditions. You can read how to establish these conditions in *Simplicity: Notes, Stories and Exercises for Developing Unimaginable Wealth* by Mark Burch; and *Developing Facilitation Skills: a Handbook for Group Facilitators* by Patricia Prendiville.

Chapter Eleven

FINAL THOUGHTS: THE IDEAS, THE PEOPLE AND THE BIGGER PICTURE

As I write this final chapter, I am trying to anticipate your reactions. It is impossible to know how a reader will engage with a book. I am hoping that you will feel empowered to take action in your own life, after reading the stories and suggestions here. I am also hoping that you haven't found me too prescriptive when I have made suggestions for taking steps towards balance and alternative ways to live. But books take on a life of their own after publication, and an author can never know how her books are experienced, so I have to let go of the ideas, which don't belong to me anyway, and send them out into the world.

The People You have Met in this Book

My biggest concern is your reaction to the people whose stories feature in the previous chapters. When I had written the first draft of this book, I gave it to several readers, whom I called "critical friends", whose constructive feedback was very useful. One of the insights they provided was that there is a danger that the stories told in the book could come across as smug and middle-class. My main reason for mentioning this is that I am afraid you will judge the story-tellers too harshly.

It is very tempting to judge as smug anybody who says they are happy and have what they want. In fact, it's almost required in contemporary Ireland, given our dominant culture of cynicism. I interviewed each person or couple for between one-and-a-half and three hours. I didn't know any of them well beforehand, although a few were in my circle of acquaintances.

They all struck me as extremely thoughtful people, who were questioning and searching, although they had of course also reached some solutions that they were happy with. They hadn't all started their lives as middle class, although they could all be described thus now, by virtue of their education, work and interests. They were aware of their privilege, and the cultural advantages that they possessed. They knew that their experience and resources opened up networks and options that many people don't have.

They told me their stories in fairly structured and rational ways, emphasising the benefits of their situations. They referred to their anxieties and difficulties, but they did not emphasise them. Nevertheless, these are present in the stories, if you read carefully. If we had had longer to discuss the complexities of their solutions, or if they had had the opportunity to come together to reflect as a group, more of these complexities might have emerged.

After each interview, I had several pages of transcript, which I had to reduce to less than 2,000 words. I worried that I did not do justice to my interviewees. When I had completed a story, I sent it to each person or couple for checking. Some made minor changes. Some remarked that they felt embarrassed, or that they were worried that they would come across as extremely self-centred, even though I had asked them to talk about themselves. One interviewee pulled out altogether, feeling too vulnerable.

The stories are simply snapshots in time and it would be unfair to assume that they represent their subjects completely. It is very brave to allow one's story to appear in print, fixed forever, for potentially thousands of people to read. And for an author, it is a huge responsibility to commit somebody else's story to print.

So, dear reader, be gentle with the people you have met in this book. Take issue with the ideas and with the way that I have written about them, but be generous in how you read the stories, because the interviewees have been generous in offering those stories in response to my request. Take what you can from them, but don't make the mistake of thinking that they are trying to tell you how to live. They are telling you what was working for them, at the time they were interviewed in 2001/02. Circumstances change, and what worked at one time may not always be appropriate, so it is quite likely that they may make changes in the future.

Some of them told me that their own friends considered them a little self-satisfied, which may well tell us as much about the friends as about the interviewees. Friends and acquaintances alike often assumed they had financial resources they hadn't told anybody about. Some certainly have more financial security than others; indeed, some have reached financial independence. Others, though, are far from financially independent and must continue to earn money. Others have very small incomes by current standards, yet they manage well because they are financially intelligent.

They all have a picture of what their life work should be, based on their current priorities, dreams or passions. Most of them do paid work, and sometimes it's connected with an aspect of their life work, sometimes not. But it's not the main event in their lives. Many who have young children have made the children one of their top priorities. But it doesn't stop there. They are also, to name just some of their other roles, learners, activists, artists, spiritual beings, friends, good neighbours, family members, and community members.

They have all responded to what Duane Elgin calls "the push of necessity and the pull of opportunity". They have worked out what matters to them and questioned the consumerist orientation of contemporary Ireland. They are not opposed to possessions, but they think very carefully about what they need, and what they are prepared to do to acquire what they need. They are able to have a good time without a surfeit of things. If they decide they need something, they are prepared to do without, until they can afford it. They have questioned norms that say we need a range of trappings in order to get on in life. They are often sceptical about conventional ways of doing things, but they avoid cynicism, and have learned to understand the world in creative ways. They make mistakes and errors of judgement, but their guiding philosophy is that of enough.

A sense of control of their lives is a common feature of the story-tellers. This has brought them reasons to be happy. Their happiness is not some unrealistically perfect thing, disconnected from the complications of the everyday world, but it arises from their experiences of choice, empowerment, purpose, and freedom.

I think of them as ordinary heroes. Ordinary, because they are people like you and me, who sometimes have money worries, work concerns, complex decisions to make and frustrations with life in general. Yet they are heroes, because they have expanded our ideas of what is feasible in contemporary Ireland. Their lifestyles are expressions of what is really important to them. Their lives are all very different, evidence that there are no blueprints for balance and fulfilment. They have not reached some kind of nirvana of perfect happiness. But the important thing is that they have taken action towards creating balanced and fulfilling lives. They do not wait for institutions and leaders to do things for them. They realise that nobody else is going to shape positive futures for them.

What If Everybody Did It?

What kind of world could we have, if everybody subscribed to a philosophy of enough and we all revised our attitudes to work and money? It takes a strong moral commitment to develop and act on a philosophy of enough, but if we did, our society could move beyond the inadequacies of both the traditional and modern worldviews that I have described in Chapter One. Economic slowdown would take place, but this would not be detrimental to wellbeing. We would devise a number of different ways of working and we would also create conditions for improved civic and political literacy, and for equality, both in intimate relationships and on a local and global scale.

We could spare the workers and the planet

If we worked, produced, sold, and consumed less, the economy would slow down. We are often told that this would eventually result in economic collapse, because businesses would not thrive, and employees would be laid off. But a deliberately chosen turn away from a society of ultra-consumption could result in steady-state or stability economies. Anders Hayden points out that we would spare ourselves, by reducing our working hours, and spare the planet and the environment, by reducing our consumption. The turn need not be accompanied by a large increase in involuntary unemployment. If citizens consumed less, they would need to earn less and do less paid work. This could lead to a situation of serial employment, which would continually open up opportunities for paid work. Local economies would also thrive, because we would have the time to support local enterprises.

Another common argument against economic slowdown is that labour productivity decreases in tandem with it. If productivity decreases, the competitive position of companies also tends to worsen. On the other hand, it is also true that if average hours of paid work fall, the rate of hourly productivity rises, as people tend to work harder or more efficiently over a shorter space of time. Governments can also take a successful proactive approach to productivity, by investing heavily in education, research and development.

Doing less paid work would allow more people to do their life work. Much of this work would concentrate on people, so there would be more educational, social, caring, cultural, environmental, health-related and interpersonal activities, which promote a strong society. There would be less emphasis on producing things. There would be no shortage of paid or unpaid work, if we operated out of a philosophy of enough, but it would be needs-oriented rather than oriented towards the satisfaction of desires created by advertising.

Mindful markets could thrive

We would have the time to find ways to preserve the advantages of markets, as outlined by David Korten. Alternative economics is not against markets, but it is opposed to the free movement of capital around the globe, and the constant pressure to produce more, without regard for the social and environmental consequences. In *The Post-Corporate World*, Korten outlines the characteristics of healthy, "mindful markets". They use life rather than money as the standard for evaluating economic choices and performance. Those who make the decisions meet the full environmental, human and social costs of business decisions. Such markets favour human-scale, local-ownership businesses; they strive for full disclosure of information and are regulated to avoid extremes of wealth and poverty. They also encourage the sharing of knowledge and technology, and are self-reliant and diverse. Communities have the ability to manage their borders so that flows of cross-border trade and capital are not all in one direction. Finally, mindful markets are ethical, and subject to due legal process. Clear and enforceable rules ensure that profit is not made from the misery or loss of people or animals or the degradation of the environment.

Conspicuous consumption would become unfashionable. The emphasis would be on quality rather than quantity. Large houses and cars would no longer be symbols of success, but of waste. Small but aesthetically pleasing and comfortable homes would become the norm. Unnecessary car use and large cars themselves would be seen as harmful. Walking and cycling would be more pleasant, and public transport would be valued, with a consequent improvement in standards. Duane Elgin writes that "a revitalising civilisation will be characterised by greater balance between material excess and material impoverishment, between huge cities and small communities, between massive corporations and smaller companies, between highly specialised work roles and more generalised work roles, and so on".

We could be active citizens

Some commentators say that if we set limits and worked with a philosophy of enough, we would become a society of happy robots, all satisfied with less, without initiative and content with low standards. In fact, both poverty and affluence already have this effect. Poverty, which is involuntary, is degrading and demoralising, and often isolates people and communities. It can make people dependent and it is often a source of social disintegration. But the affluent also become dependent. Much of their spending is passive, robotic and addicted. The affluent demand more "consumer choice", but don't exercise choice in other areas of life. They become closed off from the rest of society, either in their cars or their homes or their private clubs and compounds, at home or abroad. They tend to become dependent on private security. They are afraid to take risks.

"If we are totally absorbed in the struggle for subsistence or, conversely, if we are totally absorbed in the struggle to accumulate, then our capacity to participate wholeheartedly and enthusiastically in life is diminished," writes Duane Elgin. The philosophy of enough could not be more different from affluence or poverty. It facilitates an active engagement with life, and an active, connected and politically literate citizenry.

The questions about the future of our society are complex, and demand more than simplistic answers, but the people you have met in this book and those who feature in other studies[5] are living testimony to the possibilities for engagement, proactivity and responsibility. They contribute to a strong society, even if that is not the primary reason for their choices, simply by being more available to other people, by having the time to be better neighbours, friends, lovers, parents, grandparents, aunts, and uncles. Many also take a more active role, and become involved in voluntary

---

[5] *Choosing Simplicity*, by Linda Breen Pierce; *Getting a Life*, by Jacqueline Blix and David Heitmiller; *Downshifting* by Polly Ghazi and Judi Jones; *Voluntary Simplicity*, by Duane Elgin; *The Overspent American*, by Juliet Schor.

organisations or community initiatives of one kind or another. They are helping create the social conditions that facilitate active citizenship, where people participate in shaping their social, economic, cultural and political lives. Because their way of life is voluntarily chosen, it contributes to self-esteem and engagement with other people. People who live like this demonstrate a striking self-confidence. They are able to meet challenges and take risks. They do not depend on others to lead them, or to solve their problems. These are the kinds of citizens we could have, if everybody "did it".

We could all enjoy multiple roles without suffering overload

In a culturally creative society, people would have the opportunity to take on several different roles, as carers, earners, learners, travellers, artists, teachers, to name but a few, rather than to specialise as the current economy demands. But they would be able to maintain balance in these roles, and not become overpressed. They would thus be able to explore the multiple nature of human experience and identity, and in the process discover new things about themselves and others, as well as constructing new ways to live in and to know the world. They would have time to pursue self-knowledge, intellectual and spiritual development, and to understand their emotional responses to other people and to events, to develop emotional literacy as well as political and civic literacy.

This would create the conditions for democratic intimate relationships. Peer relationships and co-parenting, which are psychologically healthy for everyone involved, would become the norm. Every adult would understand the importance of both unpaid work and paid work. This would lead to the integration of lives, rather than the current compartmentalisation. Gender relations could be transformed, with men identifying more as fathers and domestic workers and women letting go of the control that they often feel they must preserve in the domestic sphere. Parents would have the time to negotiate decisions and the solutions to problems with their children, rather than dictating outcomes.

A reappraisal of work, career and life work would also combat the idea that life has appropriate "stages", depending on one's age. It would eliminate the countdown to retirement at 65, which has become common. It would not be fashionable to be busy all the time, at certain stages of one's life, and then to have stages for "taking it easy". The world would be more people-friendly, not just family-friendly.

Who is "everybody"?

When we think of "everybody", we need to start with the world's high and middle-income groups, who have the most consumer power, but who exist in a world where half the population has never made a telephone call. The consumer class is concentrated in the highly industrialised regions. The way of life of this class is depleting the world's raw materials, yet their affluence exists in the midst of poverty. And this consumer class is also setting a standard to which many less affluent people aspire.

In one sense, it is a highly elitist suggestion that already privileged people give up high-powered jobs and the high-consumption lifestyles that go with them, in order to create a better life for themselves. But in another sense, it would be an enormous change if the consumer class developed awareness of these issues and began living with purpose, clarifying their priorities, consuming only what they need, avoiding meaningless jobs, and devoting time to their families, relationships and communities.

Thoughtful members of the consumer class are in a position to lead the way towards a shift in values. The affluent cannot expect the poor to live within their means and shun materialism, if they do not act out these principles in their own lives. On a global scale, alternative economists such as Herman Daly insist that sustainable development must be promoted and developed in the North before countries of the South are expected to participate. So in many ways, the responsibility for taking action towards sustainability at a micro level rests with the affluent high-and middle-income groups of Northern countries such as ours.

Enough would mean less for the affluent group, but more for others, which would help to close the gap between rich and poor, both locally and globally. This would also create the conditions for strengthening democracy. David Korten points out that a viable democracy needs a ceiling and a floor with regard to the distribution of wealth. Subscribing to a philosophy of enough is actually a moral commitment to a more equal world.

The choice to live consciously and with clear moral priorities is not limited to the financially advantaged. The search for happiness is not the prerogative of a financial elite. It is true that many people from low-income backgrounds do not have the range of options that middle- and upper-income groups have, options created by social contacts, membership of networks and educational qualifications. But those on low incomes can also choose to recognise the damage inflicted by consumerist culture and untrammelled economic growth. It is important to distinguish between people with low incomes and those who live in poverty, without the means to obtain basic food, clothing and shelter. As long as we are not living in poverty, we can all learn to make intelligent use of our time and our money. If everybody did this, it would contribute towards changing our culture, so that it became unacceptable to be wasteful of scarce resources, or to be affluent in the midst of poverty.

We could have a new politics

The new political paradigm is based on the image of healthy human development and a whole-life economics, which values far more than production and consumption. In this view, a successful society is one that places the physical, social and spiritual health of the people above all else. To summarise, the new politics:

- Understands that the personal, the political and the planetary are inextricably linked.

- Understands that economics is relevant to all of the people of the earth.

- Promotes active citizenship and the understanding that economics is something that we all create, not just something "out there" over which we have no control.

- Values and protects the natural environment and fragile ecosystems.

- Appreciates the limits to growth and promotes the concept of enough.

- Appreciates qualitative issues such as happiness and well-being.

- Values relationships and connections between people and community, whether international or local.

- Is committed to egalitarian relationships between women and men.

- Is committed to egalitarian relationships between white, Western nations and people of colour and non-Western cultures.

So Why Isn't Everybody Doing It?

When citizens worry about the over-materialistic values being transmitted to children, the downsizing of companies in the name of efficiency, the destruction of the natural environment, the long working and commuting times often demanded to keep the economy growing and the consequent lack of time for self and relationships, the dominant paradigm tells them there is no alternative if we are to survive in the competitive global economy. Indeed, Richard Douthwaite points out that that is largely true, because of the ways that many countries, including Ireland, are locked into trade agreements — our government has little choice about how the economy is run. Because of global trade agreements, governments are required to run their countries in very specific ways. If they don't, international investors will cause a financial crisis by shifting their funds elsewhere. Within the present political and economic system, then, there is little choice. But the system cannot continue indefinitely, because it depends on and is depleting natural and finite resources such as oil and gas. It also has personal, psychological and social consequences which many people consider unacceptable.

Nevertheless, people who critique the present economic system are dismissed in the popular media either as hopelessly optimistic nutcases or as anti-social wasters, who do not contribute to or care about the welfare of Irish society. Those who denigrate a philosophy of enough are deeply committed to the dominant economic paradigms and, as Donella Meadows puts it, "a paradigm is not only an *assumption* about how things are; it is also a *commitment* to their being that way". There is an emotional investment in a paradigm because it defines one's world and oneself. This resistance is one of the many cultural conflicts that accompany radical change.

Public debate about economic and social issues is dominated by a simplistic either/or mentality, which creates resistance to critique. We are encouraged to believe that we have to be either traditional or modern. The media largely ignores creative alternatives. This results in a situation where many people think that working with a concept of enough is regressive and that it is about going back to a traditional way of life, such as the 1950s in Ireland. Although we can learn important lessons from that time with regard to self-sufficiency and local economics (see Richard Douthwaite's book, *The Growth Illusion*), society then was not based on ideals of equality and justice, as we understand them today. In that era, few people actively chose to live as they did, and many people were frugal because of poverty and lack of choice.

Living with a philosophy of enough does mean sailing into uncharted waters, however, and it would be naïve to assert that we can know exactly how society would be transformed. We could create the conditions for greater equality, justice and sustainable economic development, but this would mean letting go of a great deal of the certainties — material and emotional — in our lives now. This is another reason why many are reluctant to embrace change — the known, even if unsatisfactory, is often perceived as less risky than the unknown.

The task is one of creating a new culture and of taking a moral stand against the either/or mentality. Many cultural creatives who work with a philosophy of enough do not realise that there are many others out there who think like they do. And for others, lack of information about culturally creative alternatives is inhibiting awareness of what is possible. Nevertheless, considerable numbers of people are engaged in creating a new paradigm, and it is important that they share their experiences. I hope that this book can contribute to that sharing.

Happiness is a Long-Term Adventure: Take One Step Today

This book advocates making choices that are different to the dominant conventions of our day. It also shows some of the ways that those choices can be made and the shapes of the lives of some people who are engaged in the search for balance.

Chances are, if you are reading this book, you are already doing things to balance your life and would like to go a bit further. But maybe you are feeling a bit overwhelmed by the bigger picture I have outlined in this chapter. Or, as you review the book as a whole, you're thinking, it's impossible. Remember the central message about planned change: start small, take baby steps. Establish your own goals and go at your own pace. Don't berate yourself when you have setbacks. But start. Only by actually doing something can you begin to balance your life. Below is a list of suggestions from which you can choose one thing to do today.

- Make a list of three things that are contributing to balance in your life at the moment. How can you maximise them or create similar things in other parts of you life?

- Name one thing that is preventing balance in your life. How can you let go of it?

- Go through a wardrobe, a shed, a cupboard or drawer. Divide the contents into things that serve you and things that take up time and space you would rather devote to something else. Decide how to dispose responsibly of the things you don't need.

- Do a financial health-check (see page 86).

- Start keeping a spending record (see page 89).

- Spend nothing for one whole day.

- Read a book or article, or visit a website, mentioned in the *Bibliography* or *Resources* sections of this book.

- Get serious about developing a personal vision (see pages 28–32).

- Write affirmations for something you want to happen in your life (see page 39).

- Talk to somebody else about one idea from this book. Avoid people who are always negative, but listen carefully to the responses of those who are likely to be interested.

- Write a description of what an ordinary week would look like in your balanced life.

The search for balance and happiness is a path along which you evolve organically. You cannot buy them, so money is irrelevant, once your basic needs are met. The small first steps you take will definitely make you feel better, but it is also the case that the more you develop the philosophy of enough, the more rewarding the process itself will become. Happiness is not simply a reward for something we do — if it were, this would imply that it is just another aspect of consumption.

What are your wants and what are your needs? The less you want, the richer you are. If you can confine what you want to what you need, you will be happy. This demands rational planning, combined with self-knowledge and an ability to make the most of the present moment. Don't be put off by setbacks. The ongoing work of balance is a pleasurable adventure. Learn to enjoy and appreciate the tension between making the most of the present moment and shaping the future.

Learn to appreciate modest things — for how can you enjoy really big things fully, if you are not practising every day at enjoying small things? Something as simple as walking, the breeze on your face, a shaft of sunlight falling in a particular way in your home, or a pleasant encounter with a shopkeeper, a neighbour, or someone you don't know — things like this are yours to enjoy when you have time to appreciate the richness of the world around you.

Be creative about balancing your life, but remember, this involves getting it wrong some of the time. Developing balance is not complicated, but it is a skill that develops slowly, with false starts, plateaus and occasional flashes of insight. You need to be patient with yourself and look on the mistakes as learning experiences rather than failures. Holding a vision takes energy and effort sometimes. In the journey towards your vision, you should not rely on the rational mind only, but also draw on serendipity and intuition. You need to be open to events and knowledge that you might never have envisioned for yourself. When you stop compartmentalising your life, you often recognise synchronicity, that process by which apparently unrelated events and pieces of knowledge can shed light on each other.

Don't let any one way of living become an orthodoxy. If you find a better philosophy than that of *enough*, explore it. Balance demands that we all review our thinking from time to time, to see how adequate it is for the world around us and the ways we want to live. Remain sceptical, but avoid cynicism. Don't believe those who say that happiness is not possible. Have decent doubt and humility, as well as confidence in your choices. You *can* engage with your world and balance your life. Start now, and you will find a whole new range of options opening up to you.

છે છે છે

Contact me

I would like to hear your response to the ideas in this book and about your efforts to balance your life. I will acknowledge any correspondence and will respect confidentiality, although I may ask your permission to use your experiences in my future writing. You can contact me at:

Anne B. Ryan,
Centre for Adult and Community Education,
NUI Maynooth,
Maynooth,
County Kildare,
Ireland.
E-mail: balancingyourlife@eircom.net
Website: www.geocities.com/balancingyourlife

BIBLIOGRAPHY

Anderson, John O., "Why We Prefer to Rent",
www.fiassociates.org/faq1/step6.htm

Blix, Jacqueline and David Heitmiller, *Getting a Life*, Harmondsworth: Penguin, 1999.

Brandt, Barbara, *Whole Life Economics: Revaluing Daily Life*,
Philadephia, PA and Gabriola Island, BC: New Society Publishers, 1995.

Bruges, James, *The Little Earth Book*, Bristol: Alastair Sawday
Publishing, 2001.

Burch, Mark A., *Simplicity: Notes, Stories and Exercises for Developing Unimaginable Wealth*, Gabriola Island, BC: New Society
Publishers, 1995.

Callenbach, Ernest, "The Green Triangle: Environment, Health,
and Money — Help One, Help Them All", *In Context*, 26:
13–14, 1986.

Capra, Fritjof, *The Web of Life*, New York: Doubleday, 1996.

Connolly, B. and A.B. Ryan (eds.), *Women and Education in Ireland,
Volumes 1 & 2*, Maynooth: MACE, 1999.

Covey, Stephen R., *The Seven Habits of Highly Effective People:
Powerful Lessons in Personal Change*, London: Simon and
Schuster, 1992.

Covey, Stephen R., *The Seven Habits of Highly Effective Families: Building a Beautiful Family Culture in a Turbulent World*, London: Simon and Schuster, 1999.

Csikszentmihalyi, Mihaly, *Flow: The Psychology of Happiness*, London: Rider, 1992.

Dacyczyn, Amy, *The Tightwad Gazette: Promoting Thrift as a Viable Alternative Lifestyle*, New York, Villard Books, 1998. (The essay on creativity is on pages 52–54.)

Daly, Herman, *Steady-State Economics*, London: Earthscan, 1991 (second edition).

Daly, Herman "Five Policy Recommendations for a Sustainable Economy", in *Feasta Review 1*, eds. Richard Douthwaite and John Jopling, Dublin: Feasta, 2001. www.feasta.org

Daly, Herman and John Cobb, *For the Common Good: Redirecting the Economy towards the Community, the Environment and a Sustainable Future*, London: Green Print, 1990.

Dominguez, Joe and Vicki Robin, *Your Money or Your Life: Transforming your Relationship with Money and Achieving Financial Independence*, Harmondsworth: Penguin, 1997 (second edition).

Douthwaite, Richard, "Good Growth and Bad Growth", *Feasta* website, www.feasta.org.

Douthwaite, Richard, "The Growth Illusion", in Harry Bohan and Gerard Kennedy (eds.), *Working Towards Balance: Our Society in the New Millennium*, Dublin: Veritas, 2000.

Douthwaite, Richard, *Short Circuit: Strengthening Local Economies for Security in an Unstable World*, Dublin: Lilliput Press, 1996. (The second edition of this book will soon be available on the *Feasta* website, www.feasta.org)

Douthwaite, Richard, *The Growth Illusion: How Economic Growth has Enriched the Few, Impoverished the Many, and Endangered the Planet*, Dublin: Lilliput Press, in association with New Society Publishers and Green Books, 2000 (second edition).

Drake, John D., *Downshifting: How to Work Less and Enjoy Life More.* San Francisco: Berrett-Koehler, 2000.

The Ecologist, Go MAD! 365 Daily Ways to Save the Planet, London: Think Publishing, 2001.

Elgin, Duane, *Voluntary Simplicity: Towards a Way of Life that is Outwardly Simple, Inwardly Rich,* New York: William Morrow, 1993, revised edition.

Elgin, Duane, *Promise Ahead: A Vision of Hope and Action for Humanity's Future,* New York: William Morrow, 2000.

Ellis, Dave, *Creating Your Future: Five Steps to the Life of Your Dreams,* Boston and New York: Houghton Mifflin Company, 1998.

Financial Independence Associates, www.fiassociates.org

Fogler, Michael, *Unjobbing: the Adult Liberation Handbook,* Lexington, KY: Free Choice Press, 2000.

Frankl, Viktor, *Man's Search for Meaning,* Boston, MA: Beacon Press, nd.

Fromm, Erich, *To Have or To Be?* New York: Jonathan Cape, 1978.

Ghazi, Polly and Jones, Judi, *Downshifting: The Guide to Happier, Simpler Living,* London: Coronet, 1997.

Giroux, Henry A., *Public Spaces, Private Lives: Beyond the Culture of Cynicism,* New York: Rowman and Littlefield, 2001.

Handy, Charles, *The Hungry Spirit: Beyond Capitalism: A Quest for Purpose in the Modern World,* London: Arrow Books, 1997.

Handy, Charles, *The Elephant and the Flea: Looking Backwards to the Future,* London: Random House, 2001.

Hayden, Anders, *Sharing the Work, Sparing the Planet,* London: Zed Books, 2000.

Henderson, Hazel, *Paradigms in Progress: Life beyond Economics,* San Francisco: Berrett-Koehler, 1995.

Henderson, Hazel, *Beyond Globalisation: Shaping a Sustainable Global Economy*, West Hartford, CT: Kumarian Press, 1999.

Henderson, Hazel, *Building a Win-Win World: Life beyond Global Economic Warfare*, San Francisco: Berrett-Koehler, 1997.

Henderson, Hazel, Jon Lickerman and Patrice Flynn, *Calvert-Henderson Quality of Life Indicators*, Calvert Group, 1999.

Hoad, Judith, *Need or Greed? Our Practical Choices for the Earth*, Dublin: Gill and Macmillan, 1999.

Hochschild, Arlie Russell, *The Second Shift*, London: Piatkus, 1990.

Hochschild, Arlie Russell, *The Time Bind: When Work becomes Home and Home becomes Work*, New York: Metropolitan Books, 1997.

Kimmel, Michael S. and M.A. Messner, *Men's Lives*, Boston: Allyn and Bacon, 2001.

Kirby, Peadar, *Poverty amid Plenty: World and Irish Development Reconsidered*, Dublin: Trocaire and Gill and Macmillan, 1997.

Kirby, Peadar, *The Celtic Tiger in Distress*, London: Macmillan Palgrave, 2002.

Korten, David C., *The Post-corporate Wworld: Life after Capitalism*, West Hartford, CT: Kumarian Press, 1998.

Lamott, Anne, *Bird by Bird: Instructions on Writing and Life*, New York and San Francisco: Pantheon, 1994.

Lane, John, *Timeless Simplicity*, Devon: Green Books, 2001.

Lane, Robert E., *The Loss of Happiness in Market Democracies*, London and New Haven: Yale University Press, 2000.

Lang, Peter, *LETS Work: Rebuilding the Local Economy*, Bristol: Grover Books, 1994.

Larson, Jonathan, "The Greatest Generation–Economics Division", www.villa.lakes.com/eltechno, 2001.

Lerner, Magda Goldhor, *The Dance of Anger: A Woman's Guide to Changing the Patterns of Intimate Relationships*, New York: Harper and Row, 1985.

Meadows, Donella, *The Global Citizen*, Washington, DC: Island Press, 1991.

Meadows, Donella, "Not So Fast", *Resurgence* Magazine, 184, www.resurgence.org.

Nordberg Hodge, Helena, "The Case for Local Food", www.isec.org.uk/articles/case.

O'Connell, Michael, *Changed Utterly: Ireland and the New Irish Psyche*, Dublin: The Liffey Press, 2001.

O'Kane, Brian, *Starting a Business in Ireland*, 4th ed., Cork: Oak Tree Press, 2001. Website: www.startingabusinessinireland.com.

Pierce, Linda Breen, *Choosing Simplicity: Real People Finding Peace and Fulfilment in a Complex World*, Carmel, CA: Gallagher Press, 2000.

Prendiville, Patricia, *Developing Facilitation Skills: a Handbook for Group Facilitators*, Dublin: Combat Poverty Agency, 1995.

Purcell, Bernie, *For Our Own Good: Childcare Issues in Ireland*, Cork: Collins Press, 2001.

Rapple, Colm, *Family Finance*, Dublin: Squirrel Press, produced annually.

Ray, Paul H. and Sherry Ruth Anderson, *The Cultural Creatives*, New York: Harmony Books, 2000, www.culturalcreatives.org

Ryan, Anne B., *Feminist Ways of Knowing: Towards Theorising the Person for Radical Adult Education*, Leicester: NIACE, 2001.

Ryan, Anne B., *How Was It For You? Learning from Couples' Experiences in their First Year of Marriage*. Dublin: ACCORD Dublin and Department of Social, Community and Family Affairs, 2001. (Available free — telephone 353-1-7043956.)

Sachs, Wolfgang, "Rich in Things, Poor in Time", *Resurgence Magazine*, 196, 2000, www.resurgence.org.

St James, Elaine, *Simplify Your Work Life: Ways to Change the Way You Work so that You have More Time to Live*, New York: Hyperion, 2001.

Semlyen, Anna, *Cutting Your Car Use: Save Money, Be Healthy, Be Green!* Totnes: Green Books, 2001. www.cuttingyourcaruse.co.uk

Schor, Juliet, *The Overspent American*, New York: Basic Books, 1998.

Schumacher, E.F., *Small is Beautiful*, London: Blond and Briggs, 1973.

Sennett, Richard, *The Corrosion of Character: The Personal Consequences of Work in the New Capitalism*, New York: W.W. Norton, 1999.

Sparkes, Russell, *The Ethical Investor*, Harper Collins, 1995.

Swenson, Richard A., *The Overload Syndrome: Learning to Live within Your Limits*, Colorado Springs: Navpress, 1988.

Thorne, Brian, *The Secular and the Holy: Person-centred Counselling and Christian Spirituality*, London: Whurr Publishers, 1998.

Veblen, Thorstein, *The Theory of the Leisure Class*, New York: Viking Press, 1967 (sixth edition).

RESOURCES

This list of resources is not intended to be comprehensive, but to give you the means to find further information about topics mentioned in the book.

General:

Céifin International Institute for Values-Led Change, Town Hall, Shannon, Co. Clare, Ireland. Tel: 353-61-365912/3. E-mail: ceifin@eircom.net. Website: www.ceifin.com.

Ethical investment, Friends First is currently the only financial institution to offer an ethical fund in Ireland. You can also contact the Ethical Financial brokerage at 39 Ardagh Avenue, Blackrock, Co. Dublin. Tel: 353-1-2780535. E-mail: ethicalfinancial@broker.assurelink.ie

Feasta, The Foundation for the Economics of Sustainability. 159 Lower Rathmines Road, Dublin 6. Tel 353-1-4912773, www.feasta.org

Fairtrade Mark Ireland, Carmichael House, North Brunswick Street, Dublin 7. Tel/Fax: 353-1-4753515, E-mail: info@fair-mark.org. www.fair-mark.org *or* www.oxfam.org.uk/fair_trade.html

Family friendly work practices: www.familyfriendly.ie

Financial Associates: a non-profit organisation which aims to help people create more personally fulfilling and ecologically sustainable lives by applying the program detailed in *Your Money or Your Life* to develop strategies for more effective use of their life energy and financial resources. Website: www.fiassociates.org

Food Co-Ops. Information is available from *Dublin Food Co-Op*, 12a North King Street, Dublin 7. Tel: 353-1-8730451.

Independent media. The Irish Independent media is a network of over 60 national and regional independent media centres, on-line at www.indymedia.ie.

International Society for Education and Culture. A non-profit organisation concerned with both biological and cultural diversity. It emphasises moving beyond single issues to make links with the more global events that shape our lives. www.isec.org.uk

Local Exchange Trading Systems (LETS). You can get information by contacting Letslink Ireland, c/o Bill Walsh, Lower Aiden Street, Kiltimagh, Co. Mayo, Tel: 353-94-81637. At the time of writing, the Letslink website had been moved or deleted, but you can also get information via The Village website at www.thevillage.ie/articles/letssystems. Peter Lang's book, mentioned in the bibliography above, is also good.

Money Advice and Budgeting Service (MABS). Tel: 353-1-6233900. For countrywide offices, consult your local telephone directory.

New Road Map Foundation. A non-profit foundation based on the principles and strategies of the book *Your Money or Your Life*, by Vicki Robin and Joe Dominguez. www.newroadmap.org

Permaculture. See www.permaculture.co.uk, www.theholliesonline.com and www.arknursery.ie

Resurgence Magazine. www.resurgence.org

Simple Living Newsletter. www.simpleliving.net/newsletter

Slow Food movement. Resists the homogenisation and globalisation of food production and promotes appreciation and respect for food, in opposition to fast food and the "24-hour culture". www.slowfood.com

Sustainable Ireland Co-operative. 159 Lower Rathmines Road, Dublin 6. Tel: 353-1-4912327. Website: www.sustainable.ie

Walnut Books, Can supply a free catalogue of books on sustainable development and related issues. The Hollies, Castletown, Enniskeane, Co. Cork. Tel. 353-23-33785. E-mail: walnut-books@eircom.net

YES! A Journal of Positive Futures. www.yesmagazine.org

Holidays and Travel:

Earthwatch sends conservation volunteers to one of 700 teams operating around the world. Costs vary depending on destinations. www.earthwatch.org.

International Voluntary Service organises schemes whereby six to twenty volunteers from several countries live and work together for anything from one week to a month. www.ivsgbn.demon.co.uk

Idealist is a useful website for volunteer opportunities worldwide. www.idealist.org

See also www.vacationwork.org.uk.

If you have chosen a country to visit, relevant guidebooks often have sections on voluntary work or exchange opportunities.

If you are connected to a church, it may have links abroad also.

Housing:

Cara Housing Association, 8 Lower Mallow Street, Limerick. Tel: 353-61-317444. E-mail: centraloffice@carahousing.com

Clúid Housing Association, All Hallows College, Drumcondra, Dublin 9. Tel: 353-1-8573088. E-mail: cluid@cluid.ie

North and East Housing Association, 54 Derry Drive, Dublin 12. Tel: 087-2603309.

National Association of Building Co-operatives (NABCO), 50 Merrion Square East, Dublin 2. Tel: 353-1-6612877. Website: www.nabco.ie

Respond! Airmount, Dominic Place, Waterford. Tel: 353-1-357901. E-mail: responddub@esatclear.ie

Rural Resettlement Ireland, Kilbaha, Kilrush, Co. Clare. Tel: 353-65-9058034. E-mail: rri@iol.ie

Shared ownership, for details, contact your local authority housing department.

The Village, Sustainable Projects Ireland Ltd, 159 Lower Rathmines Road, Dublin 6. Tel: 353-1-4912499. E-mail: info@thevillage.ie. Website: www.thevillage.ie

Threshold, 8 Fr Matthew Quay, Cork. Tel: 353-1-8726311. E-mail: info@ threshold.ie. Website: www.threshold.ie

INDEX